WOMAN *with an* ISSUE

A Mother's Memoir of Addiction, Loss, Redemption and Recovery

Angela Richey Braxton

A Woman With an Issue by Angela Braxton

ISBN: 1-59755-097-3

Published by: ADVANTAGE BOOKS
www.advbookstore.com

Library of Congress Control Number: 2006930425

First Printing: July 2006
06 07 08 09 10 11 12   9 8 7 6 5 4 3 2 1
Printed in the United States of America

My story is dedicated to my children, in order of their births: LaTesha, Winsome, Blake, Philemon, Sultan and Malachi, and to my baby that I never had a chance to know. I also dedicate my story to every mother everywhere who has or will go through the experience of losing the opportunity to raise her own child.

As long as God gives you breath for another day, there is hope for a new life.

They that sow in tears, shall reap in joy. PS. 126: 5

To the Staff at YCCIS

May God be with you and guide you in all decisions you make pertaining to children & families

Angela Richey Braxton

ACKNOWLEDGMENTS

Thank you Genelle Pfau, for believing in me without knowing my story before I placed it in your trustworthy hands. Without you, this may not have made it into print. I am grateful to you as a co-worker and a true friend. I placed my life in your hands through my story and you never changed toward me or judged me. I thank God for our paths' crossing.

Thank you Tommy Vann for being there always, and for remembering some of the things that I just couldn't seem to put together. And for listening endlessly without judgment and encouraging me to "Go ahead with yo bad self." I love you, my friend.

To Debbie Bevier for going through so much with me even when tragedy touched your life, not once, but four times. The losses you have endured have only helped to make me stronger and to realize that after God, family is the most important thing in this life. Thank you for all the support and encouragement that you've given me. And most of all, thank you for being my sister. Love you, girl.

I thank you Robert Greer (Plowboy) for loving my sons and being the father they never had. You opened your heart and home to them out of love, and for that I am forever grateful. Although things didn't turn out the way the way I planned, I know in my mother's heart that no matter what, my boys were truly happy with you as their father during their short time with you and they will never ever forget you and all that you taught them. Thanks for your support in writing this and loving me through all the craziness I've brought into your life. I love you. And I hope you find this more interesting reading than *Smokey the Plow Horse*.

To Kenny and Rosemary Smith: there will never be enough pages in any book for me to say how grateful I am to the two of you for taking in my four oldest children LaTesha, Winsome, Blake, and Philemon. After already raising your own family you both could have done anything else with your lives but you made the decision to raise my children. I know things haven't always been well between us as parents, and I'd like to say that I'm sorry for any part that I ever played during any discord in our lives. God knew what he was doing when He placed my children with you two wonderful parents. I know it's not been easy, but you never gave up. I am forever grateful and I love you both, not only for what you've done, but for who you are.

A very special thank you to Corey, Cody and Kenny, Jr. for sharing your parents with my children, and for accepting them and loving them as your siblings.

Thank you to Calvin and Nancy Boldridge for trying to help my family and me all those years ago. I believe that your many prayers for me over the years have been answered. I love you both.

Thank you, Chrise, my dear sister, for the late night typing to get this manuscript ready. I don't know that it could have happened without your help, and of course at the last minute, as it usually is with me. Thanks for being there, helping me to make this possible. I love you.

Thank you, Anne for accepting my manuscript and causing it to shine with your editing. I am so glad that our paths crossed. You have kept me focused on the task at hand when I wanted to move forward to the end before the beginning was complete. You are truly a blessing to me. And thank you, Gary for introducing me to Anne and giving me the encouragement to see this through; there are not enough words for me to express my gratitude.

Please forgive me if I left anyone out. It was not my intent to do so. I thank you, love you and now I must get this to print!

Finally, I would like to thank all those who looked at me funny, smirked and said, "Yeah, right" when I told you I was writing my story. You gave me more determination and courage and strength to get through this than you'll ever know.

May God Bless and keep you all.

It is my firm belief that once we realize that nothing we do can make God leave us, we are free to forgive ourselves and move on. We pull our feet out of yesterday's failures and have hope for God's blessings today. You see, all we have is today.

FOREWORD

I believe that in sharing my story with the world, I can help those who have no hope and also help to promote the new Systems of Care, letting the parents of children know that they are not alone. Coming where I come from, by supporting the system in this new endeavor, I hope to help ease other parents' doubts and mistrust of the child welfare system (which I know as S.R.S. and have referred to as such throughout).

I am now the Chairperson for the Family Advisory Council in the state of Kansas. We are here in support of families but also to help child welfare workers know what families' needs are and how the workers can help families rather than hinder them. The Systems of Care approach brings parents into a decision-making partnership with child welfare, far beyond anything I experienced as a mother involved with S.R.S. Both child welfare and parents are held more accountable, with both working to ensure that fewer children are permanently removed from their parents and that parents do better at keeping their children safe and secure.

For those of you who work within child welfare systems, including the ones I was involved with, please, as you read, keep an open mind and do not personalize any of this. This is not about any of you. This is my story, and it must be told.

Some of the names in this book have been changed or no name used at all in reference to my life story. In writing this, my intent is not to hurt or cause pain to anyone mentioned but to allow my story to give hope to those in despair. Names have been changed or left out to protect the anonymity of those persons directly or indirectly involved. This story is only about me and the way I lived my life. It's the truth through the eyes of the little girl in me, then through the woman I was becoming and am today.

PREFACE

It was a Sunday in May, 1997. I stood in the pew of the church, tears rolling down my face. I somehow knew right then I would never be the same when I left the church that day. The minister was asking that everyone come forward and give all their worries and cares to God, and He would heal them. I didn't believe what the minister was saying; I thought it was just a normal part of the service. But I felt a warm tingling sensation through my whole body and I just couldn't stop crying. The minister kept urging people to come forward and I just knew that he was speaking to me.

All I could think about was how miserable my life was and how out of control it had become. I continued to cry as my feet began to move and I made it to the altar. As I fell to my knees and started thanking God and asking for forgiveness, the warming sensation was still there. The minister stood by me and said, "Give it all to God. Turn over everything and everyone, and God will heal you and take care of you."

I called out my addiction to crack cocaine and alcohol, and saw my experiences rolling by like a picture show. I called out the names of my children, all six of them, and I saw their faces. I called out the abusive relationship that I was in and I saw that man's face. All the while I was crying and begging God to heal me. And as I did, I could feel the weight of all I carried lift from my body, my heart and my soul.

I believe that the Holy Spirit moved in me that day and that it is by God's wonderful mercy and grace that I haven't used drugs or alcohol since. There were so many times that God tried to reach me and I didn't even notice. It's funny how God sometimes has to hit us over our heads for us to realize that all we have to do is ask, and it shall be given. I left that service a new person, and I knew in my heart that God was with me and would carry me through, no matter what lay ahead.

Chapter One

My name is Angela and this is my story.

I was born May 28, 1965, in Atchison, a small town in Kansas just west of the Missouri River, to Mary Lou and Herbert Richey, Jr. My grandparents are Mary and Ellsworth Boldridge and Viola and Herbert Richey, Sr. I was the last of five children to be born of my parents' marriage. In order of their birth my sisters and brother are Lynn, Aileen, Wil and Eve. My siblings and I were all born two to three years apart.

Although I wouldn't know until much later in life, there were some rumors started about the time I was born that I wasn't my father's child. It was said that my grandmother started this rumor. I knew nothing about this until I was older and had already had my first child. The man who was said to have fathered me told me about the rumor. At the time he said he believed he actually was my father, but later said that he wasn't and that I should believe my mother. He was my dad's best friend whom I had always seen as an uncle.

When I asked my mom about it she denied it, and my dad said he didn't know anything about it. I was totally shocked to hear that this rumor had been around for years. This could very well be part of the reason that the stable family of my early years did not last. One thing I am certain of is that the man that I know as my father will always be my father to me.

When I was about two years old, my mom and dad moved our young family to Kewanee, Illinois. My dad got a better job, and I think my mom thought it would be a good idea to move away from my grandmother. She and my mom didn't get along very well, and my grandmother had a big influence on my dad, who was something of a "momma's boy" according to my mother. My father's brother, Uncle Jimmy, also lived in Kewanee.

He and his wife were really nice and fun to be around. I remember that Uncle Jimmy was something of a clown and loved playing jokes.

Kewanee was another small, typical Midwestern town. Life was good for us kids in Kewanee. We had swingsets, a kiddie pool for me and a bigger one for the older kids, bicycles, and plenty of toys. I am told that, as the youngest, I was spoiled rotten by all. My dad even brought home a playhouse for me one day. I thought it was a real house for kids – it was that big. All the neighborhood children came to play in our yard, because we had everything a child could want.

We usually got all that we asked for at Christmas. We knew early on that Daddy was Santa. According to my parents, one Christmas my sisters and brother were so excited about all the gifts under the Christmas tree, they just couldn't wait. Since I was the youngest, they figured that if they had me open the gifts, none of us would get in trouble. So on their orders, I unwrapped all of the presents. Believe me, they got in trouble.

Some of my favorite early memories are of the time I spent in my playhouse. I had a kitchen set in there and my best friends Terry and Monique and I would make and eat ketchup and mustard sandwiches, believing ourselves to be quite the little cooks. Sometimes we'd go to Terry's house and his mom would fix us peanut butter and jelly sandwiches. But we liked making our ketchup sandwiches the best. That's all we knew how to fix.

One special day stands out in my memories of my father from back then. Daddy took me to Black & Fletchers, a big hardware store that sold just about everything, from tools to toys. They had some nice bicycles, and Daddy said it was time for me to have one. The one I chose was red with a white stripe and it had training wheels to start out. I was so excited about that new bike!

Daddy took me home and was teaching me how to ride it. Terry came out, saw my new bike, and he just had to have one too. A couple of days later, his dad brought him one home. Monique didn't have a bike, but I let her ride mine. She came from a very large family without much money. I remember that she was one of the few kids who, other than for church or school, went barefoot.

I loved going to Monique's house. Her mother could really cook. Mama would say, and Daddy too, "Don't be down there eating, because they have too many mouths to feed." But her mother just treated me like one of her own and always made a place for me at the table. I also liked to go to church with Monique and her family. Everyone was so happy jumping around shouting to Jesus. At first I just sat there, then I started jumping and shouting too.

All in all, my first years were all any child could ask for. I had a loving family, favorite playmates, and a sense of security and well-being that I have never experienced since. I don't think that anyone in my family would ever have guessed how quickly this would all end.

In 1968, my only brother suddenly passed away at the age of six. Wil went into surgery for a simple tonsillectomy and never woke up. I believe to this day that his death is what caused my family to fall apart. My parents were grief-stricken, and we were all stunned. Wil and my sister Eve were especially close; when he died, a part of her went with him. I know that Lynn and Aileen also loved him dearly.

As I was just three when he died, my only memories of Wil come from pictures I have of me with him; the only physical memory I have is of him in his casket. I remember touching Wil and trying to wake him and Mama taking my hand and moving us on. I still wonder after all these years, why I can't remember my brother in life.

I'm sure that before this happened, my parents had the usual arguments and disagreements, and my mother wasn't always the best of mothers. She yelled a lot, and sometimes we felt like we had to walk on eggshells around her. One thing I do know is that, despite her shortcomings, Mama loved all of her children and would gladly have given her life to save any of us. But I think she just became so angry after Wil's death that she didn't know what to do.

After my brother's death, all I remember is bitterness and anger in our house. I recall being fearful most of the time. I think I was so afraid because everything had changed; there didn't seem to be any happiness in our home anymore. Two years after Wil died, my parents divorced. I think that the pain of his death was too great for either of them to handle, and it drove them apart. They took it out on each other. My mother started drinking heavily and neglecting the house and us kids, and my dad seemed to just turn into himself. At the time they split up, I don't think that either of them had any idea of the effect their divorce would have on the four girls they still had left to raise.

Chapter Two

I'll never forget the day we left Kewanee and Daddy. Mama loaded us up in the car to head back to her childhood home in Atchison, Kansas. She was fussing and cussing all the while she packed us and our things into the car. I remember feeling carsick for the whole ride, which took about eight hours. I always got carsick whenever we made the long ride to Atchison to visit. but I think it was even worse that day. We were leaving my dad and the only home I knew to live with my grandparents until Mama could find us a place of our own.

Once we moved in with my grandparents, life settled down again, at least for the months we stayed with them. I have some good memories from that time. Grandma and Grandpa Boldridge had a farm with hogs, chickens and cattle and big combines and tractors. They had ponds to fish in, although I didn't take to fishing too well. I was afraid of the fish, and I certainly didn't want to catch any. But my grandmother taught us all. Once a fish actually got on my line; I threw the whole pole into the water.

We all loved going into town with Grandpa. We got to ride in the back of his pick-up truck, as this was back in the days when it was still legal to pile a pack of kids into the back. My Aunt Emma's kids would come down from Topeka in the summer and we'd all get into everything and cause a lot of noise and ruckus. Those were great times. We made us some stick horses and we'd ride them down to the pond and sometimes over the hill from the pond to the creek where our parents used to swim as kids. The creek was supposed to be off limits, but we'd go there anyway.

After about six months, we moved to my uncle's old house about a mile from my grandparent's farm, as my uncle had moved his family to another Kansas town about forty-five minutes away. I was glad we didn't move into town because I loved living in the country. Plus, I didn't want to move far from my grandparents and my cousins.

The Boldridges are a very big family in the town of Atchison and Atchison County. People could see any of us just about anywhere in the county and know that we were Boldridges. I liked that feeling of belonging that came with being part of a family that had made their home in one place for generations. The Boldridges were one of the oldest black families in Atchison County.

I most certainly missed my dad and my dear playmates Terry and Monique, but I was happy being in the country. It was so peaceful and everything seemed so fresh. I still remember Grandma and Grandpa getting up before the chickens, the smell of bacon and eggs cooking, and the screen door slamming as Grandpa headed out to do his morning chores.

Once we moved to my uncle's old house, we scraped by financially. Sometimes Mama worked at jobs as a nurse's aide or cleaning other people's houses,. But none of her jobs lasted long, and sometimes we were on welfare. And then there was the $100 Daddy paid each month. I am grateful that my father sent that money on a regular basis, but it was still tough on my mom raising four girls. Grandma and Grandpa helped whenever they could and sometimes when they probably shouldn't have.

After about a year, Mama started going out with two of her girlfriends from her younger days, Sylvia and Norine. Sylvia was divorced and had a son and daughter and was a schoolteacher. Norine had two sons and lived next door to Grandma and Grandpa Richey for awhile until she and her husband divorced and she and her sons moved into a smaller house.

We four girls spent a lot of time at one or the other of their houses while my mom and Sylvia and Norine went out partying. They would go out to the clubs in St. Joe, Missouri. I remember hearing them talk about all the fun they had. When the moms left, we'd play music and dance and have our own little party. There were eight of us kids, ages five to fourteen when this arrangement began. Norine's younger son and I were the youngest. My big sisters Lynn and Aileen and Sylvia's son were our babysitters since they were the oldest.

Every time Mama left, I wanted to go with her. I think I felt a little bit abandoned each time she and her two girlfriends waltzed out that door, and I knew they wouldn't be back until after I was asleep. And the older kids always picked on me when she left. They knew that I was afraid of the dark. We'd all be in a room playing, and they'd catch me off guard, run, turn off the lights and shut the door and make scary noises. All I had to do was turn the light back on, but I was always too terrified to move.

I remember that I used to wet the bed too. I don't know when it started, but it went on for a long time. I think I was too afraid to get up so I just slept right through it. I was always teased about that too. And I would get in trouble and sometimes get a whipping from my mama. The only times I remember not peeing in the bed was at Sylvia's house. Although I was much younger, whenever her daughter had a slumber party, Sylvia always made sure that I was invited and included in the party until Sylvia went to bed. Then I had to go to bed too. But she had a nightlight and would wake me up to go to the bathroom. At the time I felt very special to be included in parties with the bigger girls, but I know now that I was invited along with my older sister Eve so that Mama would have an all-night babysitter for me.

Sometimes my mom, Norine, and Sylvia would all get us kids together and take us to nearby Warnock Lake, and we'd all swim and have a picnic together. Mama hated for us to splash her because she couldn't swim and she never wanted to get her head wet. But we did anyway, and always had a good time, so long as Mama was in a good mood.

It was hard for my mother trying to raise four girls on her own. It always seemed like she was searching for something or someone to take care of her and us. But back then, and maybe even now, no man was looking for a woman with four kids. And as soon as one of the men she went out with acted like they didn't want to be bothered with us, she was done with him anyway.

There were a lot of men in and out of our lives throughout my entire childhood, starting from the time I was five. One in particular I absolutely hated on sight. He was Norine's brother, who saw himself as a real so-called city slicker straight from "Cow Town," which is St. Joseph,

Missouri. Every time he came around, the first thing he would do is take my mother to the bedroom. Neither of them cared that we were there, right in the next room. That whole deal always made me sick to my stomach and angry, so angry, that I would go out on the step and sit in the freezing cold crying until my fingers and toes went numb. I hated him and I hated her for leaving us as if we didn't even matter and going in that room with him.

I was about eight or nine years old during this time. I remember wanting to live with my dad to get away, but he had remarried and our new stepmother didn't want us children from my dad's first marriage around. She didn't like us and we didn't like her. We called her "Fat Pat the Water Rat." That wasn't very nice, but when my dad wasn't around she called us "little nigger bitches." We'd tell my dad, but he didn't believe us.

My dad is a reserved quiet kind of man and seems to do all he can to avoid confrontation. I know that he cared about us, but it was just too hard for him to stand up to his wife in our defense. We went back to visit him in Kewanee for a couple of summers but that soon ended. We'd spend time at Grandma Richey's, who still lived in Atchison, but she was always fussing and yelling about this or that. Out in the country with my Boldridge grandparents or else rubbing my Grandpa Richey's back while lying on his bed was where I found peace. My grandfather had been crippled for about seventeen years and was bedridden most of the time, but he was a very kind and loving man.

Chapter Three

I still don't know why, but when I was about eight years old, the moving began. One good thing was that at this point my mother, who had developed quite a drinking habit, stopped drinking alcohol. I like to believe that it was after I found a bottle of J&B Scotch in her dresser drawer and drank until I passed out drunk on her bed that she stopped. I'm not sure what made me drink from that bottle; I think the fact that it was hidden away made me curious. I started sipping and sipping and the next thing I knew, I was waking up with a terrible headache.

Unfortunately, once my mother quit drinking, the bad moods that used to come and go became worse and lasted longer. I know now that even if you quit drinking, if you do not change your attitudes and behaviors, you're just a "dry drunk." And that is a most miserable state to be in. For everyone around you, it's like tiptoeing around waiting for a volcano to erupt. And when it does, everyone in its path has hell to pay. That's how it felt with my mother. I almost wished she hadn't stopped drinking.

First we moved to Topeka, where two of my aunts lived. My mom wasn't very close to them but we spent time with them off and on.

In our first year, I probably went to every grade school in Topeka. I don't know how I ever passed a grade, but I somehow managed to do well in school, keeping my grades up in spite of the continual moving and adjusting to new schools. By the time I'd get settled, we would move to another side of town. I don't know if my mom couldn't keep up with the rent or what, but thank God none of her boyfriends moved in.

At first I'd make friends in my new schools to have someone to play with, as my sisters were getting older now and really didn't have time for me. Mama was either working or chasing some man, and took little notice of what was going with us girls. But after the first couple of moves, I became a loner. It was easier than making friends one week and leaving the next. The older we all got, the more alone I felt.

When I was about ten years old, I finally did get to spend more time with my mom alone, but it sure wasn't the kind of attention I'd hoped for. We would sit in the car at Johnnie's Body Shop. We were always either waiting on Johnnie to complete a car or waiting for him to show up. And if he didn't show up, we went looking for him anywhere she thought he might be. If we didn't find him, we'd end up right back at the shop, waiting.

Even though my mom and I were together, her mind was never on me. I was restless; sometimes we would sit there for hours on hours just waiting for Johnnie, and he'd never show up. Whenever she did find him, Mama would cuss him out and would sometimes beat him up. It was so embarrassing to see her that way.

My mother became pregnant by Johnnie. And then things got even worse. She started chasing him down even more. Her plan was to force him to be responsible for the baby she was carrying, but the more she chased, the more he ran. I sometimes wonder if she got pregnant to trap him.

Although I felt sad and hurt by my mother's lack of attention, I never thought that she was a bad or uncaring person. She was and still is known for her generosity, and would give her last dime to anyone to help them. My mother has a heart of gold. I just don't think she ever used it to love herself.

I was going to school with the same clothes on sometimes because our laundry wasn't done. I had the longest, most beautiful hair, but it was hardly ever combed. My sisters wouldn't take the time and Mama was either chasing Johnnie or doing something else. I didn't know how to do it myself. And it was so tangled that, by the time anyone would try, I'd scream and holler cause it hurt so bad.

And of course we had moved again. I was at a new school and even if I wanted to make friends, nobody liked me because my hair wasn't combed and I wore the same pair of green jeans all the time. I could play tetherball though. I took out my frustration and anger by hitting the crap out of that ball.

We came home from school one day and we knew immediately that something wasn't right. No matter how bad things got, my mother always fed us. We could look in the refrigerator and see nothing, but when it was time to eat she always managed to cook a full course meal. That day when we came in, she was in the bed and when we tried to get her up she wouldn't wake. I think that Lynn was there and called an ambulance.

My mother had what I was told was a "nervous breakdown" and had taken an overdose. At the age of ten, I really didn't know what that meant, but it was a terrible feeling, seeing my mother taken away in an ambulance. And she was still pregnant. I don't remember how long she was gone, maybe a week or two. I can't even recall where we stayed.

When my mother returned, we moved back to Atchison, back to my uncle's old house in the country. But we didn't live there long. We moved back and forth so much, I almost thought home was Highway 59, the road between Topeka and Atchison.

When my mother's water broke we were living in Atchison. She'd gone into labor early and had to have a C-section. At some point during surgery they thought they might lose her and called my grandparents. We were with them while my mom went to the hospital. I remember getting a lump in my throat and feeling so afraid that my mom might die.

Mama survived and gave birth to Christopher, who was small but healthy for the most part. I had a new little brother, but my mom was still very sick and had to stay in the hospital, I think for more than a month. During that entire time, I really don't remember any of her sisters showing any concern for us or my mother except for Aunt Claudine, who took care of me and my baby brother until my mom came home. She was kind and gave hugs and told me not to worry, that my mom was going to be alright. All I heard from the others was, "What are we going to do with all of these kids?"

That's when the realization hit me that they looked at us as different than themselves. They always acted like they were better than us and I never understood why. I will carry that attitude of theirs to my grave. Sometimes it's better to just knock the shit out of someone than to allow the disgust and hatred toward another come out of your mouth.

Aunt Claudine stepped up to the plate and took care of me. My older sisters were teenagers and didn't need a lot of looking after, and we were all staying at my grandparents' home. Aunt Claudine lived in Topeka at the time, but she stayed at my grandparents until my mom got home. It was like she understood what we were feeling and also knew what we had been through. She knew that it wasn't our fault that we needed help from a caring adult. When my little brother came home, she took care of him as well.

It was Aunt Claudine who taught me how to keep myself clean and talked to me about getting older and my needing a training bra because I had bumps on my chest and it was time to cover them. I will never forget how much it meant to me when she took me out and bought me matching bras and panty sets. She made me feel so special and wanted.

My mom finally came home and we remained in Atchison for a little longer. It took her awhile to fully recover but once she did, it was back to Topeka, where she went back to chasing Christopher's father some more. I could not then and still do not now understand why she did this to herself and to us.

Finally, after four more mostly miserable years, the spell that Johnnie had on my mother was broken. And at long last the constant moving ended. We were back in Atchison. I was in junior high by now, but it seems that I had skipped all the stages of getting there. I wanted to be back in grade school having friends to play with at recess. That would be lost forever.

However, things went very well for me at first. I tried out for every sport, cheerleading, and drill team. I made it onto the drill team and had drama class and band. I played the clarinet. Although I couldn't practice much at home because mama didn't want to hear the noise, I was pretty good. I tried out for majorette and made it. I was proud to be the first black majorette in Atchison. Everyone always said I was light enough. I'm not sure how I felt about this, but most of the blacks thought it was a race thing and I was light enough to pass for white. When our picture was in the newspaper, marching and leading the band, some said they couldn't tell me from the white people. I was just happy to be doing something so important to me.

As I joined more activities, the cost of uniforms and such became too expensive. Mom's friend Sylvia helped whenever she could, but she was also raising her two children alone. I always wanted Mama to come to the different functions at the school, but she never did. My mom made sure we had clean clothes and good shoes for our feet, but she just couldn't manage more than that. I eventually dropped out of band, drill team and majorette.

It seemed the only time I got attention from my mom was when I got into trouble. At this point, even negative attention was better than none. I started talking back to the teachers and getting into fights with other kids at school. One of my cousins and I were always fighting. I got kicked out of school for weeks at a time. I remember being angry all the time, and feeling like I didn't belong anywhere.

By this time, Lynn had left home and was out on her own. Aileen, Eve, Christopher and me were with my mother. Christopher, who was four years old by now, went to live with one of my aunts for awhile because it was too much for my mom to take care of us. I remember wishing they had taken me too. It seemed that once Christopher was born, all and everyone's attention was on him. But even after Christopher was gone, my mom didn't seem able to focus on me and my sisters unless our bad behavior made her pay attention.

I ended up getting kicked out of school, I think for the rest of the school year, which landed me and my mom in court. She told them she couldn't do anything with me. The court removed me from home and took me to a place called TLC in Olathe, Kansas. It was a group home. I didn't know what to expect, and it was kind of scary at first. But I actually made some friends. I used to sing a lot and the girls there used to love my singing, though I can't hold a tune in the shower now. Although I was away from my family, I didn't mind being at TLC. There was structure there, and I really didn't have that at home.

I did a little better in school while I was at TLC until another girl and I ran away. I think I ran with her because I thought she was cool and I wanted to fit in; I had no idea what I was doing. We didn't get far before I got scared and called for the staff to pick me up. She kept running.

I ended up going back home after that. Nothing had changed. I eventually got back into school and did alright for awhile. Then something happened, and I really didn't care much about school after that. One night while mama was out partying or at work, about four different guys from around Atchison, who we all knew as casual acquaintances, came into our house and started grabbing and then actually raping my sisters. Everything was crazy, and I was so panicked I didn't know what to do. I started beating them with a broom, telling them to get out and leave my sisters alone. My sisters were screaming and crying, but the rapists wouldn't stop. I ended up calling the police. The police came, but the rapists were gone by then, and the cops acted like it was no big deal to them, though somehow they reached our mother.

When my mom came home, instead of comforting my sisters, she was pissed and started cussing and yelling at us. At first it seemed that she was actually blaming my sisters for what happened. However, she ended up believing my sisters and pressed charges against the guys and we all had to go to court. We were all shocked at what happened then. The lawyers on the rapists' side made my sisters look like whores and the charges were dismissed.

After the court proceedings, I overheard my mother talking about what all had happened with another friend of hers that lived next door to us. I'll never forget my mother saying that I would go behind the house down the hill with boys. She didn't even know me, because she certainly hadn't taken the time. Little did she know, I was still a virgin until about a year later. While my mom was asleep in our house with her boyfriend one night, a friend of his crept into my room and raped me.

It was a terrifying experience. I didn't even know what was happening. It hurt so bad that it was like I was outside of myself watching what was being done to me. I had to throw up and his breath smelled like alcohol and spearmint gum. I never told my mother for fear of what she would have called me. I hate spearmint gum to this day.

Chapter Four

We eventually left Atchison and moved back to Topeka when I was fifteen years old. Sadly, my mother never understood that feeling good about your life wasn't about where you lived, it was about how you lived. Everyone always thought that they had to get out of Atchison to be somebody. What I realized later in life is that you can move anywhere, but if you don't change with that move, you're just moving all your shit to another place.

My mother remarried. I was happy about this, as her new husband was a very nice man, although he drank alcohol every day and my mother couldn't stand his drinking. I would say now that he was an alcoholic, but he never mistreated my mother or me (my sisters were all out on their own by then).

I went to Highland Park High School for awhile, but we eventually moved to Auburn, right outside of Topeka. My step-dad's niece, who was sixteen, the same age as me, moved in with us. She already had a baby but she was determined to finish school and make something of herself. And she did. We drove to Topeka High to school every day in my step-dad's car or he would drop us off. She knew a lot of people there, but I didn't fit in well. That's when I first realized that with the black girls there was a problem with me being too light-skinned. I was called "high yellow bitch" a lot. And I fought every time.

You know, during slavery times light-skinned blacks were what was called "house niggas." We got the jobs in the house, while the darker-skinned slaves worked the fields. I never expected this resentment to still be present all these many years later in my own high school.

I don't remember ever feeling or thinking that I was better than anyone, no matter the color of their skin. I tried to be friends with everyone I came in contact with. I just didn't fit in. My boyfriend was very dark, but I wasn't good enough for his family.

I started hanging out with the kids in the smoking area. I never really formed any great friendships with them either, but I had someone to talk to and feel like I belonged with. I also started drinking alcohol in the smoking area at school. Then I started skipping classes and going to the liquor store right up the street from the school. They knew we were underage, but sold to us anyway.

My grades were failing at this point and I knew there was no way that I would graduate with my class the following year. I dropped out and went to take my GED before I forgot everything. I passed the first time. Since I didn't have to go to school anymore I thought I was grown. I had just turned seventeen years old.

Chapter Five

I still lived at home with my mom. My drinking began to be an every day thing. I would steal the car after my mom went to sleep, and three of the girls I had started drinking with and I would sneak into the clubs and party all night. One night when we were out, I met a guy who was really nice, but about six years older than me.

Richard was a soldier at Fort Riley. Back then, every girl's parents told her in no uncertain terms not to get involved with a soldier, because he'd be there one day and gone the next, or it would turn out that he had a wife and family somewhere else. But of course, I thought that my situation was different, and I thought I was in love.

Richard would come to Topeka, or I'd steal the car and go to Fort Riley. He never knew that I was stealing the car and I never even took him to meet my mom. He never questioned me about meeting her; he knew he was too damn old to be messing with me.

Richard always treated me like a lady. Every time we were together, he made me feel so special. I fell in love with him. One day shortly before he returned home to New York, I had taken the bus down there for the weekend, and we were at the bus station waiting for my bus to come to take me home. That day, my heart was broken into a million pieces. Richard informed me that he had a girl back home, and that he loved her and was going to marry her when he returned.

I was devastated. Not only had our whole relationship been a lie, but Richard was also leaving forever in just a few days. My bus came, and I cried all the way home.

It would be years before I had a man who treated me with the love and respect that Richard did. Although I was hurt by what happened, I never could really be angry with him, because while I was with him, he never mistreated me and he never did anything that I didn't consent to. What hurt so badly was that he had someone else at home and in wanting me too, was too selfish to tell me this.

Needless to say, my days of dating soldiers were over. I never heard from Richard again or went out with another soldier since.

Chapter Six

After the soldier phase of my life, I started partying more with my only three friends, drinking to drunkenness daily. One day my mother and I drove past a liquor store on the way home, and a guy yelled for us to stop. I talked her into going back around the corner, To this day I don't know why, but something about him caught my eye. That's how I met Stephen, the man who would become my first child's father.

We started seeing each other. The only thing we really had in common was that we loved to drink. I was mainly a beer drinker until I met Stephen, but I eventually started drinking harder stuff. A few months after we met, the very first time we had sex, I got pregnant. And I was taking the pill. When I told Stephen, he immediately said it wasn't his. That was our first break-up; I told him that if he was going to deny this baby now, then when it was born he could continue to deny it.

When that happened, something in me changed towards Stephen. I was still living at home and he was also living at home with his mom. As I look back, I think they all thought that I lied about him being the father. I didn't know what to do, but I knew I wouldn't have an abortion. I got a job at a nursing home and worked as long as I could. Stephen found some really good jobs, but never stayed at them for longer than two weeks.

Two months before my baby was supposed to be born, I kept feeling like I was constipated. I'd sit on the toilet, but nothing would happen. Finally my mother started asking me what was wrong. When I explained it to her, she said I was probably in labor and we should go to the hospital. By this time my pain was pretty great, and it turned out she was right. I was in labor. I was also afraid because it was too early. I was terrified that I would lose my baby.

When I first learned I was pregnant, I wasn't sure if I wanted to keep the baby. I didn't know anything about being a mom. But by this time, I was looking forward to having someone that I could take care of and love, and someone who would always love me back. Months before she was born, I already loved this baby.

Stephen had finally come around. He knew that I hadn't been with anyone but him and that this was his baby. The day I went into labor, he was right there at the house already, and volunteered to drive me and my mother to the hospital. There was ice and snow on the streets that day. Not long after we pulled from the driveway and starting heading down the street, we slid into a ditch. By this time my mom and I were hysterical, but Stephen made it out of the ditch, and off to the hospital we went.

I was in labor for sixteen hours. LaTesha RaShawn Jennings was born on January 10, 1983, four months before my eighteenth birthday.

Chapter Seven

The doctors were afraid that the baby's lungs weren't fully developed and that she was just too early to survive. LaTesha had to stay in the NICU nursery for about a month. The hardest thing to do was leave her at the hospital when I was released a few days later. I felt so different; I was now a mother, and that little life was dependent on me. I went to the hospital every day. Stephen came too. He loved her on sight – he's the one who chose her name.

I'd stand at the window and cry because I couldn't hold my baby; I could only touch her hand for the first week or two. She was so tiny; she weighed four pounds, three ounces at birth and she lost weight in the first week. I was planning to breastfeed, so the nurses had me pump my breasts and bring the milk to the hospital. But by the time I was able to try to breastfeed LaTesha, my breast were starting to dry up, so I ended up bottle-feeding instead. I was truly disappointed, because everyone said breastfeeding builds a stronger bond with mother and baby and I wanted that for us. But it was a wonderful feeling to finally get to hold her.

Stephen and I had to gown up before we could go into the nursery since it was a sterile area and there were other sick babies there as well. It felt more natural to Stephen to hold our baby and feed her and change her diapers then it did for me at first. I think that was due to the fact that he had several nephews by this time and had already been doing the feeding and diaper changing thing.

I was so happy bringing my baby home. She was like a little doll, only she was real, and I loved her more than anything I finally had someone to love that belonged to me and no one could take her away – so I thought Stephen and I were getting along at that point, and I was hopeful that we would stay together. We finally got a place together and tried to make a home for our little family. We would both work for awhile, quit and work some more. Stephen continued his same pattern; he would work two weeks and quit or get fired.

I wanted more for myself and my child. I enrolled in cosmetology school and worked in the evenings at Holiday Inn waiting tables. The tips were good and somehow, we always made ends meet. Things were looking up, or at least that's what I thought at the time.

We'd go to Stephen's sister's house a lot, and that's where I was first introduced to cocaine. I had been with Stephen for more than a year now, and had not realized he was shooting dope And here I thought I was grown.

I started out just snorting a few lines of cocaine whenever I was at Stephens sisters house. I was afraid to do anything more, and I loved drinking beer. At first, I was nervous going over to his sister's house. I guess I knew in the back of my mind that things were just not right. I think the snorting came easy because it helped me fit in somewhat.

Stephen was a very jealous person, and when we'd drink or do some coke we would always end up fighting. He always thought another man was looking at me or flirting with me, or me with him. In their jealousy, one thing men never realized about me was that I never had a desire to be with more than one man at a time.

But I soon found out that Stephen was the one messing around. The level of trust that I had for him went out the window and I began to feel suspicious of him all the time. My goal from then on was to take care of my baby and me and get through cosmetology school. I graduated and went to work at one of the best black beauty salons in Topeka at the time. We even fought about that. I think he knew that he couldn't hold a job and didn't want me to hold one either, since he was the man.

Although we never married, I still thought it was important for my child to grow up with her father. But our lives together only became worse. One New Year's Eve, when we'd been together for two years, we were invited to a party at a club in Kansas City. After that we went to someone's house that Stephen knew. It was snowing pretty hard that night and the roads were too bad to make it home. This was the night that I would smoke crack for the first time. I can only wish now that it had been my last.

I didn't even know how to smoke it. There were quite a few people at this house and they were smoking it in glass pipes. One held the flame, the other held the pipe, and all I had to do was inhale. I wasn't sure how I was supposed to feel, and I'm still not sure what I did feel that night. I'd already had a lot to drink. However, I knew I liked the feeling it gave me. After that night, I'd smoke crack a few times a week. When I smoked, I could relax and talk better with people, or so I thought.

But things only went downhill with Stephen. We got to where we'd tear up the whole house fighting. He might or might not come home at night and we'd fight about that. I knew it couldn't last.

When I finally took Tesha and left, Stephen had been out drinking most of the night. The only reason I didn't go is because we didn't have a babysitter. I was asleep when he came home. I heard a noise like a spraying sound, and then I smelled urine. He was pissing in the corner of our bedroom, instead of the toilet. I just watched him. I couldn't believe it. When he squatted down as if to do the other, I went off and beat him all the way to the bathroom with a belt. We fought clear until the next afternoon.

I wanted to leave, but Stephen wouldn't give me the keys to my car, even though I had paid for it. I went to the pay phone to call my mom, who was living in Leavenworth by then, about sixty miles away. I told her that I couldn't live like this anymore. My mother came and picked us up that very day. I left everything but my baby and our clothes and never went back.

Chapter Eight

Tesha and I moved in with my mother. By that time, she had already divorced and remarried again. My mom seemed finally to have settled down with a man who was good for her. And he seemed to really care for her, and her children, even though we were grown. He was my favorite of my two step dads.

Tesha was three years old when we left her dad. I had high hopes that I could do better for Tesha and myself away from him. Stephen would come visit or take her for a weekend here and there, but he was never consistent. He never paid any child support or made an effort to help raise our daughter.

I got a job at a beauty shop in Leavenworth working on commission. My mom took care of Tesha while I worked. Things went alright for awhile, until I found out that the guy that owned the place was abusing drugs. He became more and more strung out, and I eventually had to run the place on my own until he used up all of his money on drugs and lost the shop.

I then got a job at a J.C. Penney Styling Salon. This was a much better job for me. I had an hourly wage plus commission, while at the other job I only got commission. I was still drinking alcohol but I hadn't used any drugs since moving to Leavenworth. I knew from my using in Topeka that if I kept playing around with crack it would be the end of me. I liked the way it made me feel too much for my own good.

After about six months in Leavenworth, I started dating a guy, Billy, who was very nice and respectable. We'd go out with my sister and her boyfriend. We would do simple things, like taking walks in the snow. I have always loved the snow, and Leavenworth is the oldest and most beautiful town in Kansas when it snows. Snow brings on the appearance of purity.

Tesha loved Billy. He would play with her for hours. After awhile, just when things were going really well with us, I started getting calls at the beauty shop from a girl who said she was pregnant by him. My heart fell at this news, and I asked Billy about it. He claimed that he had only slept with her once and he wasn't sure if the baby was even his.

I told him about me getting pregnant with Tesha the first time her dad and I slept together. And in the other girl's favor, I knew what it felt like for a man to claim that the baby isn't his. We started having problems after that and things only got worse. We argued about her every day. I didn't want to lose him, but I also had been where that girl was, and I didn't want her to feel like I had felt. I started seeing less and less of Billy, and he eventually started seeing other women. I went by his apartment one night and there was another girl there. I walked away and never looked back.

A friend of mine lived in Leavenworth and we'd sometimes ride up to Atchison together to visit old friends and family. She called me one day and asked if I was going to Atchison when I got off work. I told her I was, and that she and her kids could ride along. Not more than half an hour later, she called back, hysterical. Her earlier call had been from a pay phone at the store where she had gone to get food for her kids. She had left the older children at home. When she got back home, her house was on fire and the children were inside.

She lost a son and daughter that day and there was nothing I could do to help her. I was at the shop alone, and didn't have a key to lock up if I left. I felt so helpless. I only pray that she has forgiven me for not being there when she needed me most.

While we were living with my mother in Leavenworth, she and Tesha became very close. I was gone a lot, and my mother spent most of that time caring for her. Plus, I think the peacefulness and security that Tesha felt at my mother's home was a big part of it. Her dad and I would fuss and fight so much, that she never knew what would happen next. She'd been through a lot in her three short years.

I have to admit that, though I was happy to see Tesha so happy and secure, I was jealous of their closeness, and not only because she was my daughter. I also felt that my mother gave her all the love and security that I didn't get when I most needed it. But with the path that my life would eventually take, I was – and still am – grateful to my mother for being a granny to my daughter in every sense of the word. Maybe it was my mom's way of getting it right this time.

To this day, she and my mother have a bond that I will never have with Tesha. And that saddens me every day of my life. But we also have our own special bond, a love for each other that never fails.

Chapter Nine

My mom and her husband ended up moving back to Atchison. My stepdad owned a house there, and Tesha and I moved with them. At first, I drove back and forth to Leavenworth for work, and then I got a job as an instructor at a cosmetology school in Kansas City, Kansas. The job was great. I found that I loved teaching students to do hair. If only I had stopped drinking.

When we moved back to Atchison, I started staying out all night and partying and drinking even more. Hanging out with friends, I think I was just trying to belong somewhere, anywhere. I still got up and went to work, but I'd have to have a drink in the morning to make it there. And then after work, just to make it back to Atchison.

I became so dependent on alcohol that I honestly believed that I couldn't function without it. Two friends of mine and I would go to the club almost every night. Gloria didn't drink like Aaron and I did; she was always the level head among the three of us. But Aaron and I used to get so drunk that we would literally crawl up the hill to get home.

We always got into fights, most times just me and Aaron. Usually, they were stupid drunken arguments over nothing. One night we were so drunk that Aaron and I woke up in the bed together, and the bed was wet. I don't know to this day who peed the bed, but I know we didn't do anything else. I wasn't his type, and he wasn't mine.

But we were all the best of friends anyway. I love him and Gloria. They were always there for me, even if we were rarely sober together. I think they understood me better than anyone during that time in my life.

After we had been back in Atchison for about six months, my mom and I agreed that I needed to settle down, get my own place with Tesha, and start being more of a mother to my daughter. Tesha was so attached to my mother at that point that she always wanted her granny, and my mom would always give in and take her. Also, when you are a mother living with your own parents, they naturally always want to tell you what and what not to do with your child. Nothing you do is right. I was definitely ready for Tesha and me to be on our own together.

I found us a house to rent. We moved in and weren't there for a good month when I decided I would go out one night. Mom wouldn't babysit; she told me I didn't need to go out, that I should stay home with Tesha. But I was determined to have my fun. I got Tesha to sleep, and Aaron said he'd stay and babysit.

I went out and came home so drunk that when I went to bed, I put my cigarette out in my mattress instead of in the ashtray. Aaron was downstairs asleep and he smelled the smoke before I did. He ran upstairs and woke me, screaming "The house is on fire!" I jumped up to run into Tesha's room and my mattress went up in flames.

I was so scared that my baby was dead. I got her out of the house and ran back in and threw buckets of water on the mattress to put out the fire. I was afraid to call the fire department. I remembered what happened to my friend that day in Leavenworth when her children died. She was charged with involuntary manslaughter because she had left two of her children alone to go get food.

Tesha was fine, praise the Lord, but we moved out of that house within the week. We moved to an apartment, but once again Tesha still spent most of her time with my mom.

After the fire, I swore that I wouldn't drink again and would quit smoking. How quickly my good intentions went bad. I didn't quit smoking and by the next weekend, I was drunk again.

One night I was over at another girl's apartment on the next street from mine but within the same complex. It was a low-income housing development known to all as the "Ghetto," where our apartments were side by side like duplexes. There were a lot of people over at her house and we were listening to music, playing cards and drinking. Another girl and I got into an argument and were getting ready to fight, and I was about to swing at her (I always got into fights when I got drunk, and almost always with people twice my size). I weighed 125 pounds wet with clothes on. Anyway, I was getting ready to swing when she hit the ground. I never did hit her. I turned around, and that's when I met my next child's father.

Chapter Ten

He had knocked her down. And if I'd had any common sense at the time, I would have said, "Thanks," and kept on going. But I had to get to know this guy who had stood up for me and didn't even know me. After that night I started seeing Eugene.

Everyone told me not to mess with him, 'cause he was trouble. They told me he had killed someone. I asked Eugene about it and he explained what happened. He was charged with involuntary manslaughter but the case was dismissed. To this day, I still believe it was honestly an accident.

I should have realized the night that Eugene hit that girl, that he would eventually hit me too. He had had a not-so-pleasant childhood, and that's one thing we had in common. And we were both angry as hell. I can't fully say what his anger was about. But when we fought, Eugene fought me like he would a man. I can't remember when the first time was that he hit me, and I still can't explain why I stayed with him after that.

About two months after we met, I became pregnant with my daughter Winsome. There was some question on Eugene's family's part as to whether or not she was his. He's very dark and Winsome, a beautiful child, was lighter than me, and had hazel eyes. But Eugene never denied her. He was actually very possessive of her.

When we would get into a fight, Eugene would sometimes take off with Winsome for two or three days until he cooled off, then he'd bring her back. At first I was scared that he might never bring her back, but he always did, and he took good care of her.

Eugene was seeing other women all along, though and I didn't realize that until other kids started popping up. It turned out that he already had a newborn baby when I first met him, and sometime during one of our many break-ups he fathered two more children, all by different women. Even though he had proved he wasn't going to be faithful to me, Eugene and I continued seeing each other off and on.

When I first met Eugene, he didn't live in Atchison. However, when Winsome was about three months old, he moved in and we actually tried to make a home together. But my drinking was so far out of hand that we fought all the time. I was drinking every day. Eugene didn't have a drinking problem like I did; he was able to have a drink every now and then. He hated for me to get drunk – that's when my anger came out about all of his other women.

Eugene always told me that I was the only woman he'd been with that he could talk to about his feelings, and I do believe that he loved me in his own way. But I also think that, in his mind, he had me on a pedestal that I wasn't ready to be on. My drinking only got worse, and one day after we'd been living together for about nine months, we got into a fight and he left and moved back to St. Joe.

We broke up, I figured for good. I'm not sure if I was relieved that he was gone so that I could drink without him complaining or because it was best for me and my girls to have him gone. I started working as a hairdresser in Leavenworth again, and living back at Mom's house with Tesha and Winsome. My mom would baby-sit Tesha, but Winsome was a handful. I talked my cousin and his wife into keeping Winsome while I worked.

I still had to have the drink to get to work and another before I headed home. However, things went alright for awhile, until I started smoking crack again. Whenever I would go to pick up Winsome at my cousin's house, they always had company. There really wasn't a whole lot to do for young people in Atchison. We'd go over to each other's houses and play cards, drink, and get high.

One day I went to pick up Winsome, and the dope man was there and my cousin and his wife were getting high. I got high that night too, never expecting to eventually get hooked. It started off as fun, just something to do. My cousin's wife was a beautiful young woman. She was also from a small town and, like me, she had no idea what we were getting into.

Back then we didn't know it as crack; it was called "free-basing." We would cook our own powder cocaine and make a rock to smoke. I thought I was a big deal because I was one of the best cookers. You might still be a good-looking woman on the outside, but crack cocaine will break your spirit and you will never be the same on the inside. Getting hooked marked for them, I believe, the end of their marriage, and for me, the beginning of a living hell.

But I had yet to realize that. In my mind, I still didn't fit in and crack helped to break that barrier. I would go to work, come home, pick up Winsome and stay at my cousin's house most of the night getting high. After spending almost all night drinking and getting high, I would still go back to work in the morning.

There was a guy who would come up from Leavenworth. He liked me a lot. He was much older than me and he'd give me all the dope I wanted, just to be around me. Everyone thought we were sleeping together but we weren't. That didn't happen until about a year later. It wasn't about drugs when it did happen, and it only happened once.

He was one of the biggest dealers around. He was married, and his wife knew all along that he was coming to Atchison to sell dope. When she found out about me (I never learned how), she turned him in. And told him that she was the one who did it.

At one point during this period, I spent about fourteen days straight hanging out getting high. I couldn't stop. I was still going to work sporadically. I thought that I could justify my using by the fact that I was still hanging on to my job. I told myself that I wasn't like the others because I was working. The fact is, I was just as bad off, if not worse than the other dope heads.

While out on my missions to get high, I always seemed to run into a man whose been a trusted friend of my family since before I was born. He was a member of my grandmother's church – the same church that we were often forced to attend as children. He would always look me in the eyes and smiling, say, "God loves you, baby and so do I." Sometimes I'd see a tear in his eye. He always encouraged me to do better. He told me if

I ever wanted to talk or needed any help, to call him. And I always knew in my heart that he was sincere.

Today I believe that it was God calling out to me through him. hat I didn't know at the time is that he and my mother had been talking. He told her that one day I would tell her I needed help and she was to call him when I did. He promised her that whenever this occurred, he would make sure I got the help I needed.

You see, for years he lived on the other side of alcoholism, and he understood what I was going through. And he also knew God. I believe to this day that the simple words of encouragement that he spoke whenever he saw me at long last led me to believe that a power greater than myself could restore me to sanity. However, it took many more years for me to realize this.

Chapter Eleven

I came home to my mom's one morning to change so I could go to work. I sat in the chair and started to cry. I had been in and out and high for I don't remember how many days. I just couldn't keep it up, but I didn't know how to stop it. All I wanted was to be a mother and provide for my girls. Tesha, who was about six years old by now, was so attached to my mom at this point, that I felt she was lost to me. She was a very smart little girl for her years, who got all the love and security and stability she deserved with my mom. At two years old, all Winsome wanted was to be with her mother, no matter where or doing what. Just what I wanted and needed at her age. Winsome and I have always been close in a way that nothing can come between.

I was so miserable and ashamed of what and who I had become that I sincerely believed that my children and my family would be much happier if I were dead. My mom called our family friend that day and he came right over, just as he'd said he would. He took me to a woman's house and said he'd like for me to talk to her and that they would get me some help.

The woman he took me to see was a former U.S. Senator's wife who told me her own story and gave me an autographed copy of her book about her life as an alcoholic and a senator's wife. I realized that day that even the most influential people are not immune to alcoholism and drug addiction. I learned that it doesn't matter how or who you were raised by, if you were born into riches or if you are poor, beautiful or ugly. Addiction has no face or social standing.

When I left the woman's house that day, I was ready to give treatment a try. I was willing to do anything to get me out of the misery I felt about my life, anything to not see the look of sorrow in Tesha's and Winsome's faces when I'd come in all messed up. I was so full of guilt and shame at who and what I had become.

Entering treatment didn't solve all my problems, but it gave me a program to follow to maintain my sobriety. And it's also where I literally had a spiritual awakening.

Chapter Twelve

My first morning waking up at the treatment center was scary, and I wanted to leave. I wanted to stop using alcohol and drugs, but after getting a good night's sleep, I thought, "Maybe I jumped the gun."

I had breakfast and later had to see my counselor. It had been awhile since I'd had anything other than a beer for breakfast, and my system didn't take well to me putting something with substance in there. I felt sick to my stomach and very badly wanted a drink. On intake into treatment, the nurse asked me if I'd ever experienced DT's, which is shakes, anxiety, nervousness, etc. It all boils down to withdrawal from what your system is accustomed to your putting in. I was also asked during my intake if I used or had a problem with any other drugs. I answered, "No."

Little did I know then, but that lie sabotaged my whole treatment before I'd even begun. I felt that I just couldn't admit that I was smoking cocaine. It was bad enough that I was an alcoholic at the age of twenty-two.

I met with my counselor and together we came up with my treatment plan. I'd have one- on-one sessions with my counselor weekly or more, and attend groups throughout the day. By the end of my first week, after waking up during the night, shaking and sweating until I thought I would die, I awoke to hear the birds chirping outside.

It became very clear to me that I had shut out all things around me on my road to self-destruction. It was like waking up from a long sleep, to realize that all of nature still existed. I've always been a lover of nature with awesome wonder at how everything is nature was created; birds singing is a big part of that. And it hit me that I hadn't noticed their chirping and singing for years. This is what I call my very first spiritual awakening. This will come if you follow the steps set forth in the program of Alcoholics Anonymous to help us achieve and maintain sobriety.

It was if the scales had been removed from my eyes and ears that morning. I knew at that moment that I would do all I could do to make this treatment work for me and for my children. Although I would not fully understand the true meaning of rigorous honesty until several relapses and treatment centers later, I did complete treatment with a whole new attitude.

Of course, the fact that I never admitted my other addiction meant that I was not truly on the path to recovery. In recovery, secrets and denial keep you sick. As an addict, you cannot be addicted to one drug and not the other. You can kid yourself all you like, but if you think you can still use one drug and stay away from the other, you have already set yourself up to relapse. That's just what I did to myself when on admission to treatment, I admitted only to my alcoholism.

Near the end of my treatment, Winsome's dad started visiting me on a regular basis. Eugene was doing pretty well for himself, or so he had me believing. He had moved to Omaha. He said he was happy about the help I was getting and hoped that we could get back together permanently. He asked me if I would marry him after I got out of treatment.

I felt excited and hopeful that things would really work out for us this time. I also knew our history, and realized that, while I had made an effort to change, I wasn't certain about Eugene. But I wanted to believe that things would work out between us and that our being together would be better for me and my girls.

In treatment, you are advised to stay away from old playgrounds and playmates, especially if they were not a positive influence in your life. Even though we get clean and change, that doesn't mean that those we left out there have changed. They usually remain the same, and can't even fathom that you have truly changed. When it came to Eugene, I chose to ignore this advice. And although I wasn't honest about my drug addiction, upon leaving treatment I was determined to stay clean and get my life together and raise my little girls.

Chapter Thirteen

Once I came back home, my first mistake was being so excited about being clean that I wanted everyone in town to know that I had changed. I was so happy and proud of myself for completing treatment, I wanted to stand in the middle of the park and shout to everyone, "Hey, look at me!"

I'd see our family friend who steered me into treatment, and he would always say, "God loves you, and so do I." Whenever I saw him, he was always happy to see me. He always encouraged me to do well and make something of my life. He never judged me or looked down on me. He later explained to me that he knew when I was doing well, because my eyes had a sparkle when I was clean. And when I wasn't, the sparkle was gone.

Eugene and I wrote back and forth, he from Omaha and me still in Atchison. He said he was getting things together and that the girls and I should be able to come there soon. Marriage was never mentioned again.

I began going back around to my cousin's house and hanging around with my old drinking friend Aaron again. I honestly believe that I wanted everyone to see that I was strong enough to be around drugs and alcohol and not use. And I also think I was trying to prove this to myself.

But I still had this need to fit in and be a part of everything. And just as oil and water don't mix, neither do clean and dirty. In recovery, dirty means that you're using. Sure enough, within a few months, I had convinced myself that I only went to treatment for alcohol, and not for cocaine. Therefore I could smoke crack as long as I didn't drink. This is one of the biggest lies that addicts tell themselves.

I started smoking again, and within a week I was back to where I left off, smoking crack and drinking as heavily as I was before I went into treatment. I say "right where I left off" because you never, ever go back to the beginning. You will never get that first initial high in a lifetime of using. Yet that is the very thing that addicts chase. We used to call it "chasing rainbows."

I didn't let Eugene know that I was using again, but I think he figured it out. My return letters to his became short, if I answered at all. And I wasn't there most times when he called. I was hoping that he would just come get us, believing that if I could just get out of Atchison, that I would be alright. I honestly believed that a new environment would help me get clean again. This is where I started following in my mother's footsteps, believing that moving to another place would solve all of my problems.

Six months after I left treatment, the time came to move to Omaha. I planned on taking both Tesha and Winsome with me. Well, Tesha did not want to leave her granny. I wasn't surprised, although I really wanted her to come with us. My plan was for this to be a totally new beginning for all of us.

My mom advised me to, "Just go up there and get settled and then come back for Tesha." It did make sense, since I hadn't even been to Omaha yet. However, we both knew that wasn't her real reason for suggesting I leave Tesha with her. It would have placed Tesha too far away from her to check on how she was doing.

In the end, Tesha and Granny won their case, and only Winsome and I went on to Omaha. She was still a toddler and Tesha was in kindergarten. I decided that it made sense for me not to take her out of school. That would have made her repeat my history of so many moves through my childhood.

When we got to Omaha to what I thought would be our apartment, I was in for a big surprise. "Our" apartment turned out to be ours, along with Eugene's brother and his girlfriend, and their baby that was the same age as Winsome. Four adults and two babies in a small two-bedroom, one-bath apartment.

I knew right then that I had made another mistake. And I also knew that Tesha would never end up there with us. My heart sank. I wanted to go right back to Atchison, but the shame of having to admit I was wrong kept me from leaving then. I knew that I would leave eventually, because although Winsome was with her dad, Tesha was not with us or even nearby. Plus, I knew there was no way she would be happy up there even if I made her come. I wasn't happy myself.

About a month later, I finally met Eugene's mom. She had been living somewhere else in Omaha and ended up moving in with us, along with a teenage daughter and another one who was Winsome's age. I kept talking to her dad about us getting our own place. I got a job at a nursing home to help us save enough money to get us out of that cramped apartment.

Eugene and his brother went to work every day, but come payday there was never anything to save for us to move. Even with my paycheck, there was never enough. I even had to steal formula and diapers at times, because Eugene got to where he wouldn't come home after work, and stayed out until late at night, leaving us in the apartment with nothing to eat.

Eugene and his brother always seemed to have money to buy weed or go out and party, leaving us at home with their mom and all the kids. We began to have some pretty heated arguments, and I was ready to leave him and move back in with my mother. I had to quit my job, because lots of times he wouldn't get home on time to take me to work.

By this time, about two months after I moved to Omaha, I'd started drinking again. I had stopped again when I moved to Omaha. I guess I was trying to prove that since I got out of Atchison, I didn't need to drink. I can't remember what holiday it was, but we were going to Atchison to visit, and I packed all of Winsome's and my things, because I had no intention of going back. We were on the highway heading to Atchison when Eugene told me that I was a drunk and he wasn't leaving Atchison without his daughter. I lost it then. I went off about how he took me up there, not to marry me but to be up there with him and all his damn family, me having to steal food, diapers, and formula so we could eat because his money went, God knows where. I just went on and on. His mother was with us, and she was telling Eugene that he shouldn't let me talk to him like that.

Next I knew, Eugene had punched me in the face so hard that my head hit the car window and I thought it would explode. The hitting went on until we reached Atchison. And thinking back, I still can't believe that both Eugene and his mother, too, were beating me, right in front of my daughter and hers as well. At some point I blacked out. The last thing I remember is Winsome screaming and crying.

Chapter Fourteen

I woke up to lights in my face and a doctor asking me if I knew my name and where I was. All I remembered at the time was that I was going home. Once I was more awake, I realized I was in the hospital, and there was a doctor and two detectives there. They told me that I had been left lying in the parking lot of the Atchison Hospital. They wanted to know who did this to me. And then it all came back.

I wanted to know what happened to my baby. They said they didn't see a baby. I told them to call my mother and see if Eugene had brought Winsome to her. They called my mom, who rushed to the hospital. My face was so badly beaten that she didn't even recognize me.

Eugene hadn't taken Winsome to her, and she hadn't heard from him at all. The police tried to check around and see if he was still in town or if he had gone to St. Joe to his dad's house. But he had headed back to Omaha with my baby, and the police really couldn't do anything about him taking her because she was his child too.

They could get him for what he did to me. I tried calling Omaha, but Eugene's brother kept saying he wasn't there and I had no way of getting there just yet. I called the police in Omaha every day and they went by the apartment. But he had moved to another apartment with his brother and his girlfriend. I finally reached the girlfriend after about a week. Eugene was out, and she told me that Winsome was there and was fine. She also told me where they lived now. She said that Eugene had told her to let him know right away if I called, so I couldn't come get Winsome.

Eugene called me back after a couple days and told me that he would kill me if I came up there to get Winsome. I was afraid, because he had already killed before, accident or not. After what he'd done to me on the way to Atchison, I believed he would. I was really hoping that he would just cool down and bring her back.

I called back a week later and got Eugene's brother on the phone. I asked him if he would let me know when Eugene wasn't around so I could come get Winsome. I would let them keep all the furniture and everything that I had brought from Atchison when I moved up there. And I wouldn't call the police to have them come with me to get her and all my stuff.

I think that Eugene's brother and his girlfriend were taking care of Winsome more than her dad was anyway. So he agreed that he would let me know when I could come get her without Eugene knowing. My sister Aileen and I went to Omaha to pick up Winsome. Even though I said I wouldn't, we called the police to go with us. But they were delayed in getting there. I was feeling desperate to the point that I was going to get my baby or Eugene was going to have to kill me trying, so I didn't wait for the police to arrive.

I went in alone, and as I was leaving, heading to the car, Eugene got home. He realized what was happening, ran in the apartment, got a gun and starting shooting at us as we pulled off. I looked back and the police were just pulling up. I didn't care, I had my baby, and we were headed home. I still don't know what happened when the police arrived. The only thing that mattered to me was getting Winsome back where she belonged, with me.

After finally getting away from Eugene and getting Winsome back, I was so mixed up in my heart and my mind that sometimes I had myself believing I was crazy. I remember thinking that out of everyone I knew, my children were the only ones who actually loved me. I couldn't even love myself. The men I had been with only bullshitted me. Although I knew in my mind that they were no better than me, they always managed to make me feel worthless, and I began to believe that about myself.

Now I was back in Atchison again. What I didn't realize when I left there was that I had only been trying to run from my addiction. If you don't stop and deal with it, it will not go away.

It wasn't long before I started using just like before and even worse.

After staying with my mom for about four months, I got my own place again. I was working again but still partying and getting high. The girls were with mom most of the time.

My life was so out of control, I didn't know if I was coming or going. All I wanted to do was get high. Everyone said I needed some help, but I didn't care what they thought. I felt like shit, and this was the only way I knew how to deal with it. I had two little girls and no idea how to be a mother. Their fathers were hardly around, and when they were, all they talked about was how bad a mother I was.

About two years later at the age of twenty-five, I became pregnant with my first son. I was pregnant by a man I met in treatment. We had been seeing each other off and on after I came back from Omaha. I didn't tell anyone about my pregnancy for a long time – not even my son's dad, with whom I never had much of a relationship. I think I was in denial. I couldn't believe that I was pregnant again. I never got very big with any of my pregnancies, so I didn't have any explaining to do for awhile. I think my mother always knew, but when she'd ask, I'd tell her I wasn't pregnant.

I was so lonely during this time, and I kept to myself a lot. One day a few weeks after I'd learned I was pregnant, I was at my house lying on the couch and Winsome's dad showed up. Eugene apologized for all that had happened in Omaha and, incredibly, after all that he had done, I started seeing him again. I was so stupid.

Winsome and I ended up moving to St. Joe with Eugene. We had our own apartment there, just the three of us. I didn't tell him I was pregnant either. But the fact that I could keep this secret to myself only proved how much attention he paid to me. After our first month there, Eugene would go to work every day, come home and leave again. I was still drinking and things started to look like they had back in Omaha. Eugene's mother had moved to St. Joe as well, to move in with and take care of her grandmother, who had Alzheimer's disease.

One day after I'd been in St. Joe for about two months, Eugene hadn't come home for a couple of days, and there wasn't any food in the house. I took Winsome and we walked to Eugene's great-grandmother's house where his mother was living. I later found out from people on the streets that he had started using crack and had left town with someone else. I felt like a damn fool again. Everyone had repeatedly told me to stay away from Eugene, and I just wouldn't do it.

As miserable as I was, I couldn't go back to Atchison and face my family and Tesha and let them all know I had made yet another stupid mistake. Eugene's mom let us stay there with her. She was getting high every day, and I started smoking with her again. It got so bad that we would get her grandmother up, feed her and Winsome and her own daughter, then take the kids, leave Grandma at home and head out on a mission to get drugs for the day. I wrote bad checks from some old accounts I had, and she began maxing out all of her grandma's credit cards.

We'd start the day in St. Joe and drive to Atchison, Leavenworth, Kansas City, Topeka then head back to Atchison or Leavenworth to get our drugs. We'd either sell all the goods we bought with my bad checks and Eugene's great-grandmother's credit cards, or trade them for drugs.

This went on every day, seven days a week, until two weeks before my son was born. By then, all the checks were gone and the credit cards were maxed out. And I was starting to get sick. During a moment of sanity, I became afraid for my baby's life. How could I do what I was doing to my unborn baby? When this hit me, I knew that I had to stop and go home to my mom's. I was scared that my baby might die or come out deformed because of all the drugs and alcohol I used. If anything happened to him because of me, I don't know how I could have lived with that knowledge.

Winsome and I went back to my mother's to live. I'm not sure what my mom thought of all this. She was probably just as sick of me and my bullshit as I was, but she still took us in.

On July 27, 1989, Blake was born. I delivered him at a hospital in Kansas City, Missouri, after a very difficult labor. My mom was there with me as always. She fussed a lot, but in the end she always came through for us. I remember praying to God that if he let my son be alright,

I would stop using drugs and be a real mother to my children. I lay in the hospital bed scared to death that they would find drugs in Blake's system, handcuff me to the bed and take him away. And for what I had done I deserved just that.

When I was able to hold my healthy baby boy and look at him, I knew in my heart that I loved him, but as with the girls, I still didn't know how to be a mom. But I was determined to try my best, and to keep my side of the bargain with God, for He answered my prayer and Blake and I left the hospital together a few days later. I got another apartment in Atchison, and had Tesha, Winsome, and Blake with me.

Chapter Fifteen

Stephen, Tesha's dad, started coming to Atchison to visit her and we started seeing each other again. I always seemed to be going backward. I don't know why I couldn't just be okay by myself with my kids.

When Blake was only eight weeks old, I found out that you do not go back on bargains with God. Who was I to even think I could bargain with God? He doesn't do bargaining. It's his way or straight to hell. And that's exactly where I went that awful day.

Stephen and I had been drinking all day and I was so drunk, I passed out after putting Blake to sleep. While I was asleep, Stephen went back out. Blake woke up at some point and I didn't hear him. When Stephen came back, Blake was still crying loudly. Stephen tried shaking me awake and then finally hit me really hard in the shoulder. That woke me up, and the fight was on. The people who lived downstairs were fighting too. The woman came upstairs and asked me to call the police because her boyfriend had kicked her door in and started beating her up. I called the police for her.

When the police arrived, they also came to my house, and I was arrested right then and there for I can't recall how many bad checks I'd written. I had warrants in every county where I had written checks, five counties altogether.

I was immediately taken into custody; I didn't get to even say goodbye to my children. I thought I would get released on bond but that wouldn't happen, as I had too many warrants in different counties. What I most regret to this day about my time in prison is that I didn't get to bond with my son. Blake was a tiny baby when I left and he was thirteen months old by the time I returned home.

I started in the Atchison County jail and spent about sixty days there. Thirty days waiting to go to court and thirty more before the next county would come pick me up. Stephen had dropped my kids off at my mom's, and she looked after all three of them while I was making my way through the various jails.

He kept promising me that he was trying to get money to get me out, but that was a lie from the beginning. Stephen was messing around with some female. I later found out he had even given her a lot of my clothes, right down to my underwear! Why would anyone want to wear someone else's panties?

My mother kept trying to bond me out, only to find out that if she did, they wouldn't release me but would let the next county know to pick me up. I couldn't call very often because no one could afford to accept collect calls from jail. And neither my family nor anyone else didn't really want to talk to me anyway because of what I'd done to my children and my mom's having to take care of them.

I felt more alone than I've ever felt before or since. I certainly learned the truth of that saying, "Out of sight, out of mind." The second county to pick me up was Leavenworth. I was in jail there for another thirty days. Then came Wyandotte County. That's where I realized that I wasn't quite as ignorant as I and everyone else thought I was. There were some pretty tough women there. Most were there for crimes due to drug use, just like me. After talking with some of them, I learned that I was the only one there with any kind of real education. I couldn't believe it, but most of the other inmates could barely read or spell, and I had always been pretty good at both.

Although I wanted out of jail, by this time I knew it wasn't going to happen until I had gone through the legal process of each of the five counties where I'd passed bad checks. No one would visit or bring my kids to visit. But I really didn't want my kids to be subjected to going through a visit at a jail. It would have made things harder for all of us.

I knew that I had to do something with the time besides eating and sleeping. No one would put any money on my books (which means providing money to spend), so I couldn't even buy stamps to write my kids and mom. Finally, Grandma Sweetie, my grandmother on my dad's side, said that she wouldn't send me money but I could call her once a month and she would send me a book of stamps every month. She will never know how much it meant to me that she did that for me.

To pass the time, I taught the women who wanted to learn how to read and write. I got such a positive feeling of being helpful to others and, it was also better because there were other women I could talk to. The two previous counties only had men, so I was in a cell alone all that time.

Chapter Sixteen

When I finished the process at Wyandotte County, Shawnee County picked me up. I was there for another thirty days before going to court. It was the last jail for me in the state of Kansas. All the counties in Kansas gave me probation after I left their jails. After court in Shawnee County, I had to sign extradition papers so that Buchanan County, Missouri could pick me up and bring me to St. Joe.

The State of Missouri had ten days after I signed the papers to pick me up or I could be released from the Shawnee County jail in Topeka. On the eighth day they still hadn't came. My cell faced the front of the jail and I watched for hours, praying they wouldn't show. On the ninth day there was an ice storm. I got my hopes up, thinking that would save me. The ice was a good two inches thick everywhere and businesses were closed. On the tenth day, the guard told me if that if the Missouri car wasn't there by 5:00 that evening, I would be released. At 3:00, the people from St. Joe slid in to get me. My heart sank.

I spent sixty days in jail in St. Joe. When I went to court for sentencing, the judge sentenced me to five years in the Missouri Department of Corrections, suspended to three years because of all the time I had already spent in Kansas jails. I was devastated. My attorney had told me I would get probation because of all the time I'd already been in jail.

I wanted to at least see my children before they took me to prison. I asked the female guard when I would be leaving and she replied, "When we get a carload." She couldn't tell me when because of security reasons. When I got back to the cell pod, I called my mom and asked if she would bring my kids for a visit the next morning because I wasn't sure when I would be leaving.

I knew that once I went to prison, I wouldn't get to see any of my family. No one came to visit while I was in jail, so I knew they sure weren't coming to the prison. My mother said she'd bring the kids. I hadn't seen them since the night I went to jail in Atchison, so many months before. After talking to my mom, I went to my cell and tried to keep my spirits up, thinking about seeing my kids and trying to ignore thoughts about the prison time I would have to do. At some point I must have fallen asleep.

The next thing I knew, I was being awakened and told to pack my stuff; it was time to go. The guard left while I got my things. I didn't even know what time it was. When she came back, I asked if I could call my mom so she wouldn't come all the way up there with my kids. She refused. She then put a chain around my waist that connected to handcuffs on my ankles as well as handcuffs on my wrist. I was led to a waiting car with four men in the back seat, where I was also put.

I had never been so humiliated in my life. This was the carload the guard had told me about earlier. It was 3:00 in the morning of the day I was to see my children, whom I hadn't seen for six months. And I knew wouldn't see them for at least another nine months. In Missouri at that time, you did three months in prison for each year of a sentence. Which means I had to do at least nine months for my three-year sentence and complete the remainder of the time on parole after release.

The car took us to Fulton, Missouri, where we first stopped at a receiving facility where they took inmates before going to the actual prison. There, prison staff did medical exams and ran other diagnostic tests. They determined by your history what level of facility you would go to.

This is also where I became a number. I will never forget that number as long as I live. It's #4070. Until release, prisoners carry a card like a driver's license with your picture and that number. If I were to return fifty years later, that number would remain the same.

This was the most degrading experience I would ever encounter. But looking back, I know that God was with me, or I wouldn't have made it through.

Chapter Seventeen

There were a lot of women at Fulton, all waiting to see what prison we would be sent to. Chillicothe was a lower level prison and I just knew that I would go there. With a three-year sentence, I was considered a short timer. And believe me, I was locked up in the receiving facility with women who were facing some serious time: some had twenty to life, life plus fifty years, or even life without parole. The Death Row women at the facility were locked down for twenty-three hours out of a twenty-four hour day.

The Level 3 prison was Renz Farm. That's where all the long timers went. I couldn't believe it when I was told that's where I was going. I thought they had made a mistake because there were only a handful of women there with less than twenty-five year sentences. More than more than half were women doing life. However, the sad fact is that a lot of them hadn't actually committed the crimes they were there for, but had taken the rap for husbands or boyfriends.

When I arrived at Renz with several others, we were kept out of the general population for ninety days. This meant that we would spend those days in a basement full of cells that we shared. The only time we came up was to eat meals. I soon learned that I would have to act tough, even though I didn't want to. I made it real clear that I wasn't there looking for a girlfriend. My goal was to do my time and get out.

There are plenty of ways to add more time to your sentence once you're in prison. And I wasn't going there. I met a few honest people and when we were finally done with our ninety days, I was put in Dorm 4, which was actually a medical dorm. But I was put there because I was a short timer. I learned that the only reason I ended up at Renz was because I was considered a flight risk because of the probation in Kansas. Since I went to prison, the Kansas court placed a hold on me to be returned to them upon my release from prison for my probation, and that's what placed me as a Level 3.

In the dorm we had six by nine foot cubicles and a footlocker to keep whatever belongings we had. We were told when to get up, eat, and sleep. Unless you had a medical condition preventing you from working, we all had to work, for ten cents a day. I worked nights in the boiler room. I would measure and maintain salt levels for the water supply to the prison. It was a pretty boring job, but it helped to pass the time and I could sleep during the day since I worked nights. Although I've never been a day sleeper, my hours kept me away from having to deal with the day-to-day stuff around the prison. It was a way of not having to get too close to people, which sometimes is best in this situation. I saw a lot of women get their heads busted while I was there, being hit with a lock in a sock.

My cellmate was an older lady who was serving life for murder. She had already been there for twelve years. In that time, she had become an ordained minister, and prayed with me and the other inmates daily in our dorm of about forty cubicles. I just couldn't believe that at twenty-three years old I was the mother of three and in prison. I was living with women who had committed murder, including some who had killed their own children, husbands, or grandparents.

One day the realization hit me that I was no better than them. We were all criminals, we all had time to do. Short, long, or even life or death sentences; it didn't matter. We had all in our own ways committed crimes and the consequence had to be paid.

So I just did my time as well as I could. I don't think that I was ever really scared in prison. I was just angry and humiliated that I had ended up there. I never got to see or speak to my children. And you really don't go about making friends in prison; there is no one that you can truly talk to and confide in. Plus, everything comes with a price. If you ask for or borrow something you have to pay back double or triple. You learn early on never to ask for something you can't pay for, or you will be fighting. With most of the women at Renz locked up for at least 25 years, and plenty for life, things that we take for granted out here are like gold in there. A pack of Kool-Aid , cigarettes, soap, or lotion could all land you in a fight if you borrowed and did not pay back as agreed.

Minor infractions could get you in big trouble. One day when I was close to being released, one of the guards was checking fingernails. Fingernails that were too long were considered weapons. I couldn't believe it. I had to cut my fingernails that day or get sent to the hole, meaning I would be confined to a hot, dark space 24-7 until the authorities were ready to let me out. The count on your time stops while you are in the hole. As you might imagine, I cut my fingernails pretty damn quickly.

I made it through prison without mishap. I had a perfect record during my nine months there, and believe me that's hard to do. But I kept one goal in mind daily: that was to see my children again and hope to God that they still loved me.

Chapter Eighteen

The very day I was released my nightmare started again. The police from Topeka (Shawnee County) picked me up at Renz. I thought I would see a judge once we arrived in Topeka and then go home, but instead I ended up spending another thirty days in jail, waiting to go to court. I was afraid I would start the jail cycle all over again.

So, I was back in jail in Topeka, but also had only thirty days to report to my new parole officer in Atchison. After thirty days, I was able to go before the judge in Topeka. Upon realizing that I had just been incarcerated in Missouri, he released me, but only to Wyandotte County (Kansas City, Kansas). At long last, once I got to Wyandotte County, the judge there released me that same evening.

I couldn't believe I was finally free. My sister picked me up in Kansas City, Kansas. I was so afraid that another county would be picking me up that I was scared to wait outside the jail, so I had her pick me up at a McDonalds a few blocks away.

I thought she would have brought my children, and I just couldn't wait to see them and kiss them and hug them all. But when she showed up, she was alone. This bothered me, and she didn't say much about it on the way to Atchison.

Once we got there I found out why. My children were no longer with my mother. They were in S.R.S. (child welfare) custody and were living with my cousin and her husband in foster care. I was so excited about being released and being able to finally see them, only to find out that things had gotten so bad with my mom, that she had had to give them up several months earlier.

Although it's true that I received very few letters in prison, no one had told me that my son Blake had quit breathing one day. hank God for the Boy Scouts, where my little brother Christopher learned CPR. He literally saved my baby's life that day.

I learned for the first time that shortly after this frightening incident, my mother had a nervous breakdown and had to be hospitalized. At this point, S.R.S., along with other family members, stepped in and told her that she couldn't take care of my kids anymore. This would be my first, but far from last, encounter with the child welfare system concerning my children.

I thank God that my cousin had the children because they were with family and I was still able to see them, but it would be awhile before I got them back. After all that time away, I didn't know what to do as a mother who has been out of the picture for so long and does not have custody of her own children. Blake didn't even know me. The most horrible feeling is to hold your own child and hear him cry for his mama, knowing he isn't crying for you as his mother. And the most painful thing is having to call her to come get him, so that he can be comforted by the only mother he knows.

I had a lot of stipulations placed on me by my parole officer (PO). I had to get a job, a place to live, no going to bars, stay clean and sober and pay restitution. And report to her whenever she called. Although I was out from behind bars, my life was still not my own.

However many parole stipulations there were, they were not even close to the requirements that S.R.S. placed on me to get my children back. I had to stay clean and sober, get a place to live that met all of their rules, get a job, have successful supervised visits, the list went on and on. S.R.S. required that I have everything done in ninety days. Between the two sets of stipulations, it was almost impossible to meet all of them. And neither the PO nor my S.R.S. caseworker seemed to understand that I was dealing with not only their requirements of me.

I had been out of society for more than a year, and when I left that society, I was addicted to alcohol and drugs. I didn't have a clue as to what to do with myself, let alone finding a job, getting a place for me and my children, and learning how to be a mom.

But I was determined never to go back to prison and to get my children back. I did everything my PO and S.R.S. worker wanted me to do. I got a job at a restaurant, a place to live and went to AA meetings whenever I could. But with S.R.S. it was never enough. Although my children were spending more time with me, including overnights, it seemed like there was always something more that I needed to do to meet S.R.S. approval. The reintegration plan never stopped growing.

I had a three-bedroom apartment, and the kids had their own rooms as required. My mother and grandmother helped me with getting beds and furniture that I would need. Another cousin and his wife who are related on my mom's side, helped me as much as they could too.

I had started going to church with them. I still don't fully understand why they had it in their hearts to help me so much. The husband is my mother's first cousin and he and his wife showed me more love and concern than any of my aunts and uncles. All I can gather is that it was God who placed them in my life.

Chapter Nineteen

Leon, the brother of a girl I met while I was in jail in St. Joe, came to visit me about a week after I got back to Atchison. He wrote me constantly while I was at Renz and put money on my books quite often. He was the only person who came to visit me. He got there so late that our visit was only an hour, but at least he came. No one in my family ever visited.

When Leon got to Atchison, it was obvious that he had been drinking that day, and I knew right away that he was not a guy that I wanted a relationship with. For one thing, I had no intention of going back to drinking or drugging and the alcohol was a turnoff. But I slept with him that day. I think I felt like I owed him, because he didn't even know me but was there for me when I was in prison. But I also knew when Leon left that day that I wouldn't be seeing him anymore. I had too much to do to get my children back and I could not tolerate any type of drinking or drug use. I was sincerely trying to keep myself straight.

What I didn't know until some weeks later was that I got pregnant that day. When I found out I was pregnant, I didn't tell Leon. Although I didn't see him after that, I still talked to him on the phone. And every time I did, he was drunk. I eventually quit talking to him altogether.

My second son Philemon was born on June 29, 1991. About six months after Philemon was born, I went back into treatment. Although I had finally gotten my kids back, I had started using on and off before my new baby was born, even though I was still under the threat of S.R.S. taking my children from me. Everything had just become too much. All I heard from my case worker, mom. all that I was doing wrong, never anything right. I felt so totally overwhelmed and hopeless. I didn't feel that I could do anything right. I felt like everyone, including my family, was looking and waiting for me to screw up again.

I was still on parole and I went to my PO and was honest with her about my relapse. I had let my children and myself down again. My PO arranged for me to go to a treatment program at Osawatomie State Hospital instead of back to prison. When she said I had to go to Osawatomie, I almost said, "Never mind, I'll take prison." All I had ever heard people say about Osawatomie is that it was for crazy people. And as bad as I felt about myself, I didn't quite consider myself crazy.

My children went back into foster care, with a white family at first, them my cousin and her husband raised all kinds of hell with S.R.S. until they gave them back to their family. Thank God they did, because it later turned out that the man in that home had been molesting his children and also had molested several foster kids under their care. He landed in prison.

My first morning at Osawatomie, I woke up to someone's wild screaming. It was a scream like I'd never heard before, and clear from the other side of the hospital. It was quite far away but sounded so close. I was afraid that they had put me away for good and I would never get out. I just knew that any moment, someone would be coming to give me a shot of Thorazine and I'd begin the shuffle.

But that didn't happen. I was truly in a treatment program, and I had plenty to work on. The best thing I got out of this time in treatment was gaining self-esteem. We had a public speaking group, and each day we had to come up with something of interest to speak about. This group actually took away the fear that I had of socializing with others. I began to feel like I was a part of something positive, and like I could contribute to the group. Since then, I haven't had to have a drink to feel like I fit in.

I completed the program, and my counselor recommended that I go to a halfway house in Lawrence, Kansas for mothers with children instead of returning straight to Atchison. My PO agreed, so I had to go. I actually felt positive about this plan, and was really looking forward to the fact that after ninety days at First Step House, my children could come there and stay with me. My thoughts were that it would be ideal, because there I could take parenting classes and learn what I could about taking care of my children. We would all be there together. getting the help and counseling we all needed to get through all the mess we'd been through. And I would have the support of the staff there to help me, instead of S.R.S. and my family constantly telling me what I was doing wrong and what I could or should do about my children.

Well, ninety days came and went and S.R.S. would not allow my children come live with me at First Step House. I don't believe that this decision was because S.R.S didn't think I would be able to handle them. The reason given to me was that we shouldn't take the kids out of daycare and school, and that they were settled in my cousin's home. I believe that the plan all along was to have my cousin adopt the children. But these are only my thoughts.

I was determined to stay clean and sober and make an honest effort to get my life together. I went to work, attended AA and NA meetings and worked my treatment plan. Every now and then an organization would donate tickets to the house for different functions in the community that we otherwise couldn't afford to attend, such as concerts and plays. These were great opportunities for us. You see, most of us forget in our addiction that there are other things to do besides getting high. Recovery is like being reborn; it can feel like becoming a child again and learning to ride a bike for the first time.

One day, we received free tickets to the circus in Kansas City. I had never been before, and here I was, a grown woman at a circus, taking in all of these new and wonderful sights and sounds. It was a magical experience. We were all having a good time and at intermission we went to get something to drink. There were some guys there and we found out that they were from another treatment center. We joked around with them, and when we returned to our seats a few of them followed and sat by us. I didn't see anything wrong with them sitting with us. We were all just having fun and I really didn't expect to see any of them again. But I did.

Chapter Twenty

About a month after the circus, I was at a NA meeting, and one of the guys I had met that evening at the circus was there. C.B. said that he had completed treatment and had moved to Lawrence to a men's halfway house. I didn't think much about having run into him again, although he made it real clear that night that he wanted to get to know me better. I told him that all I could offer was friendship, since I was already seeing someone. He said, "May the best man win." I was actually quite flattered.

The man I had started seeing was someone who I'd met at a NA meeting when I was at First Step. Landon seemed totally different from any man I'd ever been with. He brought me flowers all the time, he opened my car door, and, what meant the most to me, whenever he made a promise he kept it.

But after a while the flowers began to be a nuisance. What was worse was that Landon began to break his promises. I was working at a beauty salon in Lawrence, and one day after he drove me to work, I got a call at work from a woman, telling me that she had been with Landon for years and that they had three children together. I knew he had a son by another woman who lived with him. But I didn't know about this other woman with three girls. I felt betrayed, and I realized he was just as bad as the other men who had lied to me. I was both hurt and furious with him.

When Landon came to pick me up after work that day, I asked him about the woman who had called, and he told me that they hadn't been together since before he met me. But from the minute I got that call, I was done with him. I had been with him for almost six months, and he never once thought to mention that he had any other children.

By this time, C.B. and I had become friends. In recovery, you learn to talk to others and share what you're going through. I had hoped that, as a man, C.B. could help me to understand what the other man's motive for not telling me about this other woman and their children might be. My feelings were hurt, and I think I needed someone to let me know that the games Landon played weren't about me, but were more about himself. C. B. wasn't able to help me understand the reason why Landon kept this information from me, but he did help me to eventually get past the hurt I was feeling. We also became closer and C.B. let me know that, as he had said in the beginning, he wanted more.

I really wasn't interested in C.B. in a romantic way. He was nice and fun to be around, but I was just trying to get to know myself at the time, including trying to figure out how I went from the possessive, jealous types to the slick, smooth- talking, flower toting, door-opening man with another woman and kids that he didn't feel I needed to know about. I knew that both types were just plain no good.

I really didn't want to be vulnerable to C.B., although he was always there for me and very supportive. I could call him crying and talk to him about anything. He always encouraged me, telling me, "You're stronger and better than that" and "Things will get better."

C.B. was going through a divorce, and I didn't and still do not mess with married men. That's such a hurtful thing to the party it's being done to. There are already too many home-wreckers in the world, and that's someone I'll never be.

I can only wish that C.B. and I had remained just friends. The relationship we started after his divorce became yet another possessive, jealous, drug addicted nightmare. I left First Step after a year, and C.B. and I moved in together. It wasn't long after this that C.B. relapsed, and I followed right behind. That's how most relationships with two addicts go. And it only went downhill from there.

Meanwhile, I was seeing my kids maybe once or twice a month. I didn't have a car and I could only go to see them if someone was willing to take me. Although I was supposed to be working on getting my kids back and strengthening my bond with them as their mother, S.R.S would not pay for or provide transportation. Why this was, I do not know.

C.B. and I stayed in Lawrence for awhile, then moved to Atchison. I wanted to be closer to my children and I figured that if I was right there in the same place as S.R.S, my caseworker would have to address the issue of reintegrating me and my children.

C.B and I decided to get married. Well, the truth is that he and my family decided that we should get married. My concern was that, with both us being addicts, our making our relationship permanent was a disaster waiting to happen. We actually did clean again and stayed clean until our actual wedding night, about six months later.

My cousin who I had begun going to church with, got C.B. a job making good money at a plant in Atchison where a lot of my family worked, and we did well for awhile. Everyone, including my children, liked C.B. He was a very likeable person, but that didn't really make a difference in the end. The biggest problem with most addicts is our addictive behavior, and neither of us had overcome this. And although he seemed to everyone to be a good person and a hard worker, C.B. never seemed able to stick to any job for long.

Chapter Twenty-One

C.B. could build or repair anything. He remodeled and redid the hardwood floors of the house we moved into after we married. It was a nice house. I just did not want to be married to him. I think I only agreed because everyone thought he was such a good man. And where else would I find a man who would want a woman who already had four children? Plus, now that I was married, my caseworker seemed to be more willing to work with me on getting my children back.

What everyone failed to realize is that we got high on our wedding night, and everything went downhill from there. The kids would come over for visits and overnights, and for awhile it looked like I was close to getting them back. I had quit using again; I just didn't want to get high anymore. By this time, C.B. and I always fought when we were both using and most times even if we weren't.

I dearly wanted my kids back home with me. And I wanted S.R.S. out of our lives. The only way to do that was to get myself together. I just didn't know where to start. C.B. was getting high two or three times a week, and probably more times that I didn't know about. He didn't get high at the house though, and I was glad, because I knew that I wasn't strong enough to say no if it was right in my face.

My grandmother lived right down the street, and I'd talk to her on the phone or go to her house just to keep myself away from C.B. and the urge to get high along with him. She didn't know that's what I was doing, but it helped me for awhile.

After C.B. and I had been married for about six months, I had to go into the hospital and have surgery. It was supposed to be outpatient, but I ended up having to stay overnight. C.B. was there for awhile, then he left.

He didn't show up the next morning either. I figured he had gone on to work, but my cousin called to see how I was doing and said that C.B. had called in, claiming that he was at the hospital with me.

I knew then that he had messed up. It was time for me to go home, and I kept calling the house but got no answer. My mom had to pick me up at the hospital. When we got home, C.B. was there. He had been getting high and was paranoid as hell. I was so mad, I wanted to scare the shit out of him. I didn't have to do anything but raise my voice. When people are getting high they spook real easily. C.B. hurried to the car, shaking like he had Parkinson's Disease, asking if I was alright and saying that he was just getting ready to come get me. He said he wanted to take me to St. Joe, and that he had a surprise for me.

My mom drove off. I knew C.B. was high and he knew I knew. But he had a lot of nervous energy, and I sensed that something more was going on. He didn't want me to go in the house for some reason, and just kept trying to get me into the car. I had just came home from the hospital. I told him I wanted to change clothes and he needed to tell me what the hell was going on. He was making such a big deal about keeping me out, that I really wanted to go in the house and see what was up. I was wondering if maybe someone was there who he didn't want me to see.

Well, there wasn't anyone in the house and neither was our brand new T.V. I knew immediately that he had sold it for drugs. Not only that, he had been getting high in the house, which I'd never known him to do before.

I knew that C.B. didn't have any money; that's why it hadn't bothered me when he left the hospital the day before. I told him that I was through with his shit. He had already stopped bringing home his check so I could make sure the bills were paid. I said that I couldn't live like this any more; I wanted a divorce, an annulment or whatever I could get to be done with him. I just knew that I wanted him out of my life. I was too close to getting my kids back and I told him that he had to go.

I also wasn't sure how much longer I could go on without getting high myself.

I now know that I was afraid that it would only be a matter of time. C.B. begged me to let him stay and give him another chance. He promised that he would quit using and get it back together. In the end, I gave in. I figured if I could stay clean, even though it hadn't been for long, then maybe he could figure out a way to do it too.

My second surprise that day was that C.B. had received a credit card with a ten thousand dollar limit. So we went shopping in St. Joe. He was trying to make up for messing up and selling our new T.V. I fell for C.B.'s promise not to use again, and I could certainly go for a shopping spree. I also think that the idea of my finally getting a wedding ring made me feel for some crazy reason that things might be different. He replaced the T.V. and also bought me a wedding ring. When we got married, we had only exchanged bands. We got some other things we needed for the house went grocery shopping and went home.

It was close to Christmas at the time, and on that shopping trip we also bought the kids a lot of clothes, toys, and bicycles for Christmas. The kids were coming to spend the weekend, and we were excited about being able to give them a real Christmas with everything they wanted. The kids knew we had a bunch of stuff for them, and it was hard for me not to let them have it all that weekend they visited right after we went shopping. I wish I had.

Everything went well for about two weeks. Then I woke up one morning and C.B. wasn't there. I knew he wasn't at work, because it was the weekend and he didn't work on weekends. I started to get sick to my stomach. And it wasn't just because he wasn't home. I also somehow knew that if I went down to the basement that the new bicycles would be gone – sold for dope. I didn't know it the time, but there was another reason my stomach was upset. I was pregnant again.

Chapter Twenty-Two

My children came over to spend the night. They were so excited about Christmas coming. I had told them that they were getting everything they had asked for this year.

But before they came that day, I had gone to the basement to see if the bikes were gone, and of course they were. I had no way of getting them back and no money to go get more. I was humiliated and embarrassed, and felt ashamed of myself for marrying this man and bringing him into my children's life. I had already let down and disappointed my kids enough with my drug use. And now their Christmas was going to be ruined.

C.B. came home later that night. The kids were in their beds asleep when he arrived. I told him that I didn't want him there and that he'd better figure out a way to get those bikes back. We argued back and forth,

I had stashed the only money I had under Tesha's pillow, just in case he tried to take that. When I went to look in on her and Winsome, Tesha was awake. We must have woken with her with our angry voices. The hurt that I saw on her face made me want to die. She had heard everything. I felt so ashamed. Here I was, married to and pregnant by a man who could care less about any of us.

The guilt and shame were so strong that all I wanted to do was get high so I wouldn't have to think about or feel what was happening right now. I took the money I had stashed, with every intention of getting those bikes back. When I left the house that night, there was ice and snow everywhere and I left walking. But by the time I made it to where I thought the bikes would be, I was so ready to get high that I knew before I made it there that I would use that night.

I was allowing my guilt and shame to cause me to sabotage

everything that I had worked so hard for where my children were concerned. I had let my children down again and I just gave up. I stayed out all night getting high.

The next day was a Monday. Tesha was supposed to be at school and the other kids at daycare. Instead of getting them up and ready to go, C.B. called my mom and told her that I hadn't come home. They went out looking for me and couldn't find me. I didn't want to be found. I knew that I had lost everything and I couldn't face anyone, not even myself, and especially not my children.

I believe that C.B. was more angry about me getting high without him then about my not coming home that night. Instead of calling my cousin who had had my kids in foster care, he called the caseworker from S.R.S. I know he did this just to get back at me. From the moment I found out that he had called S.R.S. to report me, I truly hated C.B. And I hated myself even more for taking on the guilt and shame for something he had done and going out and getting high over it.

When I finally got home, my children were gone. C.B. was there and I told him that I'd rather be dead than to be in the same house with him. He said that since we had come to Atchison, all I worried about was my kids and if I'd get them back or not. He said that I didn't give him enough attention. I couldn't believe this grown ass man was standing before me saying all this crap to me. hat did he expect me to be concerned about?

That's when I told C.B. I was pregnant, and asked him if he would feel the same way after I had his baby. He got all excited and tried to hug me and started telling lies about how he would change. I told him that I really didn't care if he lived or died, and at the time I meant that in my heart. How could C.B. stand there and think that because I'm having his child that everything would be alright? He had just played a part in my losing my four.

I didn't want anything to do with C.B., and I really didn't want his baby. I was too angry, hurt, and full of rage to feel anything for him or for a child of his. I wanted to die from all the shame I felt inside. All I wanted was to be a mother to my children and be happy with them, and I just kept messing it up.

I think it was a little while later that same day that my PO called. I told her that I had relapsed and was pregnant and also told her what had happened with my children. She already knew; that's why she called. C.B. had probably called her too.

I told her that at this point, I really didn't care what happened to me. She said that she thought I'd been doing really well and she was shocked at what I was saying to her. She wanted to know what led to this change. I told her everything that had been going on with C.B. and with my children, and that I couldn't believe that she actually wanted to help me. I told her that I'd be better off locked up. I didn't want to hurt my children any more. And I said I would kill myself just to get away from my husband.

By late that evening, my PO had me on my way to a treatment program at Menninger's (The Menninger Clinic) in Topeka. It was the most expensive treatment program I'd ever heard of, but my husband's insurance would pay for it. I believe that once more God was looking out for me and I still didn't realize it.

Whenever I had heard about Menninger's, it was that it was a mental hospital for crazy rich people. And I didn't think that I was crazy, I just felt like I was worthless to anything or anyone I came into contact with.

I was kept under close supervision until the staff and I both realized, through different counseling sessions, that I really didn't want to die. What I needed to learn was how to put my life back together and also deal with the fact that I was pregnant with another baby.

In the beginning, I was in denial about wanting the baby. I believed that if I didn't grow attached to him while he was in the womb, that after I had him, it wouldn't hurt so badly if S.R.S. took him after he was born. And yet, another part of me realized that my unborn baby was all I had left, I was so afraid that I would lose him too, just as I had my other four children.

At Menninger's they had never had a situation like mine. I didn't need any medication for treatment, and that's how they were used to treating people. Plus, they didn't want to give me medication because I was pregnant. Together we set up a treatment plan specific to my needs, and concentrated on my bringing a healthy baby into the world.

My stay at Menninger's lasted about ninety days. A month before I was to leave, the staff helped me start looking for treatment centers for mothers with children. At $1000 a day, my insurance was running out, but we had determined that I needed to remain in some sort of structured treatment setting geared more toward women's issues.

I was accepted at Women's Recovery Center (WRC), in Topeka, about fifty miles from where we'd been living in Atchison. It was a 30-day treatment program where women could come and bring their children. Daycare was provided and school transportation if needed, while the mothers attended groups to work on recovery issues. We had our own individual apartments within the same building and if you didn't have any children with you, you usually had a roommate.

C.B. showed up before I left Menninger's; he had also decided to go through addiction treatment there. Addicts in relationships tend to feed off each other. I was glad that he wanted to get clean but I'm still not sure if he was really sincere about it, or went to Menninger's just to keep up with me. There's nothing wrong with getting clean along with your partner, but I learned the hard way that you will not stay clean until you do it for yourself and sincerely want to change. You cannot get clean for your children, parents or material things.

If someone had offered me a million dollars at that time in my life, that wouldn't have kept me clean. With that kind of money, I would have drunk and drugged myself to death before I could even spend much of it. The program of recovery only works for those who have a desire to stop using. I did not fully understand that until I left Menninger's and went to Women's Recovery.

C.B. did get clean and actually found work and a house for us. He really didn't want me to go to WRC, but I had worked on building my self-esteem while at Menninger's and understood that I had to start taking control of my life and be accountable for the decisions I made. I was going to have another baby and I had a lot of issues to deal with. I knew that a program focused on mothers was what I needed then.

I thank God I made that decision. My treatment there was the beginning of me believing in myself. My first session with my counselor there was totally different than any I'd ever had. The first thing she made me do was identify myself. She helped me to connect with who I am, not what others expected me to be.

Drugs are not the only thing that addicts have to recover from. Most of us have to go all the way back to the beginning and work through all the things that got us to this point. And if you do an honest inventory of yourself, you're well on you way to a drug-free life. One of the biggest issues that stop women from being open and honest and asking for help is society's view of what a woman or a mother should be.

About two weeks into my treatment, I went into labor. The WRC staff was concerned that I would go home instead of returning to treatment after I gave birth. They had never had someone that close to delivering at WRC. But I was determined to complete this program. Sultan was born April 20, 1993. Three days later, my son and I returned to WRC to complete my treatment. Everyone loved Sultan, and called him the first WRC baby.

My treatment became more intense after that. I was afraid to leave and be on my own with my new baby. I didn't want to get out and mess up again. I would sit on the steps in the evening after groups and rock Sultan in my arms and sing "You are My Sunshine" to him. I promised him that he would never go through what I had put his brothers and sisters through. In my heart I meant everything I said but in my mind, I was scared to death.

Chapter Twenty-Three

I got an extension to stay at treatment for a couple of weeks longer. We had to set up a relapse prevention plan and I also had to meet with my counselor and with C.B., so he could be aware of what my relapse prevention plan was. We also needed to set up counseling for the two of us together.

I was still very angry with C.B., and probably shouldn't have moved in with him after treatment, although he was now clean and sober. We still had a lot to work on. Plus, we both needed to attend AA and NA meetings on a regular basis. We went together, even though it's not really a good idea to attend the same meeting as your spouse or partner. Part of recovery is about finding your own individuality and that's hard to do when two addicts are in a relationship.

Sultan and I moved home after completing treatment. By the time I went back for my eight-week check-up, I was pregnant again. I felt trapped. Even though I kept going back to him, I knew in my heart that C.B. was a truly bad choice for a partner and that I should have left him long before this. Any caring or trust I had ever had for him had ended when he called S.R.S. on me in Atchison. Now I feared that I would never get away from him.

I managed to stay clean and sober for about six months. C.B. relapsed much sooner, I suspect even before I got out of treatment. After we'd been living together for only a few months, C.B. was sent to jail, which was a relief for me.

I started going to outpatient treatment for awhile. When C.B. went to jail, I started hanging around with a girl I met in treatment. Soon she started using, and with her coming around me getting high all of the time,

I started getting high again too. By the time I went into labor, I was using all the time again. By then I hardly had a thing to my name, and barely had a place to live.

On May 18, 1994, Malachi was born. I had that same fear as when I had Sultan, that I would end up losing them both. My addiction to drugs was once again so out of control that I just could not stop unless I went back to treatment. But I really didn't feel like I another treatment was the real answer. I had all the tools I needed. I just didn't know how to use them once I relapsed. I always did very well in recovery for awhile, and then something would happen that hurt me or made me angry. Instead of working through it or asking for help, my response was to throw away all the good work I'd done and go get high.

C.B. had become jealous and abusive before we even left Atchison, and it only got worse once he got out of jail. I justified staying with him in spite of our constant fighting by saying and believing that the most important thing was that we were a family, no matter how messed up we were. The only time I could recall having a real family was when I was a small child, before my parents split up and we left Kewanee. I guess I was hoping that I could somehow provide that sense of security for the two boys by staying with their father even though we were worse off together than apart.

After I had Malachi, I did end up going back into treatment. At this point, treatment was an escape for me. I always worked and talked a really good program, but I couldn't walk the walk for long. My counselor suggested that I go to a longer-term treatment and seriously make some decisions about my marriage, including getting honest with C.B. about my feelings.

There were so many issues that I still had left to deal with. I told my counselor that I would do the long-term treatment this time, even though I had been in and out of treatment so many times already that if I wrote about them all it would be a never-ending treatment story. However, before I made it into long-term treatment several months later, things went downhill even further.

I finally went in to have my tubes tied, when Malachi was three months old. The surgery went okay, but on a return visit to my doctor, I complained of lots of heavy bleeding. The doctor said she wasn't sure what was going on, and ran some tests. Then she packed me with gauze, told me that she would see me again in a couple days and that if I was still bleeding she might have to do a hysterectomy.

When I returned to her office, the doctor removed the gauze packing and blood almost filled her shoes. She immediately sent me over to the hospital for an emergency hysterectomy. Everything went quickly after that. During the beginning of surgery, the doctor realized that my uterus was distended and closed me back up. When I woke up in my hospital room, I thought I had already had the hysterectomy. C.B. was also there, and when my doctor came in she explained that I was pregnant but there was no way I would carry the baby to birth. I had already been pregnant when she tied my tubes two weeks earlier. So here I was eight weeks pregnant, cut open and still bleeding. C.B. and I had to decide on whether or not to go ahead with the surgery.

Chapter Twenty-Four

A day and a half later, we moved ahead with the hysterectomy /abortion. I had made the decision to kill my unborn child. I had no idea I had been pregnant and neither did my doctor. I was later informed that it was a girl. By the time I got out of the hospital, C.B. had moved us into a nasty, filthy trailer park. That was the only place we had to go. And it was not only nasty and filthy, but infested with drugs. I could not believe that I had gone down this far. Most of the time there all we did was focus on finding and using drugs. I wasn't taking very good care of the kids, and I was so ashamed to be living there all I wanted to do was stay in the house and get high, I was also ashamed to talk to anyone about my problem.

I stayed down for awhile, until one day I got the courage to pack up the boys and leave for a battered women's shelter. Then I finally made it to Hoisington, Kansas for long- term treatment for mothers with children.

Chapter Twenty-Five

Before the boys and I left for Hoisington, I told C.B. that I would not decide about our marriage yet. My counselor had suggested to me that I not make any decisions then, so as not to add to the list of things I already had to deal with concerning my addiction. As an addict changes, lifestyle changes tend to mess with the course of recovery, and divorce is a major change.

Hoisington is way out in Western Kansas, with a population of less than 2500. I had no idea what to expect out there in the middle of nowhere. When we arrived by bus in nearby Great Bend, a van driver from the treatment center picked us up. The boys were fussy and tired because of the long trip, and I was ready to scream.

Sultan and Malachi were so close in age that it was like having twins. Sultan was a fearless little boy and full of energy. Every time he went outside or got out of the car, no matter where we were, he would take off running. It was rough sometimes, holding Malachi and chasing Sultan. Although at first I would get angry, at some point my frustration at having to chase him all of the time just left me. I realized that was his way of releasing all his pent up emotions that a little guy had no idea how to express. So instead of being upset when I caught him, we'd laugh all the way.

When we got to the treatment center, I realized that it was a whole apartment complex with something like eight buildings. We all had her own apartments, depending on how many children we had. I got a two-bedroom apartment since I had two boys and they could share. A lady delivered groceries to us every week with menus of what we could make and how to prepare the food. Anything extra we had to purchase ourselves at Hoisington's one grocery store, and at Duckwall's, the one small department store. I remembered Duckwall's from my childhood in Topeka and didn't know it still existed until I got to Hoisington.

On the grounds was daycare for the children and laundry facilities and a recreation room, which wasn't much but gave us a place to hang out and socialize while we did our laundry. And the phone was there. We didn't have phones in our apartments.

After the first ninety days of treatment, we could start looking for jobs and were expected to pay rent for our apartments. We could only work part-time because we still had our responsibilities to our children and treatment. I knew the first day I arrived that I would apply to the hospital, which was a block away.

My counselor at women's recovery had a similar history to my own. She had lost her children as well. But she got them back. And boy, was she tough, which is what I needed at the time. I always seemed to glaze over things and make them seem not as important as they really were. She said that I wore masks to hide what I was really feeling, because I believed that if people really knew what I felt that they wouldn't like me. The intensity of the treatment I received there caused the masks to fall off. Before I knew it, I was stripped naked of everything. All the past hurts, failures, guilt and shame were stripped from me.

I was able to finally see that I was a beautiful, loving, compassionate, caring woman. It was a startling thing to realize that, no matter what I'd done, I was not the worthless person that I and everyone else believed me to be.

Every day I learned something new about myself. The biggest of all the lessons was that I was and could be a mother to my children. After we got up each morning, I'd fix us breakfast, get the boys cleaned up and ready for daycare, take them to daycare, then go to my groups or work. They had lunch at daycare, and I'd pick them up after work by four or five o'clock, and we'd go home together. I'd read to them and sometimes some of the other kids would come over with their moms, I'd bake cookies, and we'd just have a good time. I prayed with them each night and taught Sultan to say his prayers. Malachi was a little too young; he was still a baby.

I had my two sons and I was determined to make it this time. I was away from everyone and all things familiar to me. I had no other choice but to look at myself and concentrate on being a mother and making a real commitment to recovery. I never felt so free in all my life.

Just as I'd planned, I got a job at the hospital, as a Certified Nursing Assistant (CNA), and was working my program, and taking care of my children. I was actually doing all the things I had convinced myself I couldn't do. I was living life on life's terms and dealing with my problems as they came along. I had become rigorously honest with myself about (almost) everything.

During one of my earlier stays at WRC in Topeka, I had been served with court papers stating that the state of Kansas was asking the court to terminate my parental rights to my four oldest children who were still together in Atchison. My cousin and her husband wanted to adopt all four of them. My counselor from WRC in Topeka agreed that she would go to court with me in Atchison. My cousin who my children had been living with was there, and my mom came to the court too. Sultan was only about three months old at the time. I remember being afraid that the state would try and take him too, so I didn't take him with me.

I had been clean for about six months by that time and was hopeful that the court would have mercy on me and give me another chance. This was not to be. My rights to my four oldest children were severed that day. The judge stated that my children deserved the stability and security of knowing that they had parents and a permanent place to call home.

I can't possibly explain the feelings of hopelessness and despair that came over me when I heard the judge's decision. I thought that I would pass out, and my legs felt as if they would just fold up beneath me. My head was spinning so bad that I felt that I would vomit up the big boulder I had in my throat. I couldn't trust myself to speak. I could only cry.

I realized the judge was right about what my children needed, and at the time, as much as I wanted to give them that permanency and security, I knew that I could not make that promise. My cousin and her husband had taken care of the kids off and on for so long, and had given them the love and care they deserved. Even though they had three children of their own, they found the love in their hearts, and space within their home and family to raise my children too.

Although it took me years to accept it, this was the best thing for the children. They were all kept together and not split up. They were raised in church, so they all know God. My two daughters graduated high school, and the oldest one has graduated college and is thinking about going to Japan to teach English for a year. Winsome will go to college in the fall with majors in music and business.

My cousin and her husband and I haven't always seen eye to eye. But they never kept me from seeing my children, and for that I am grateful.

C.B. had gone back to treatment as well, and although I didn't speak to him much over the phone, we wrote back and forth. I was avoiding making the decision to stay with him or be done with him where our marriage was concerned. My parents' divorce certainly had an effect on the rest of my life. I think I kept hanging on to my marriage for that very reason.

My counselor suggested that I start to take a look at divorcing or staying with C.B., make a decision, and stick to that decision. I had already been at Women's Recovery for about six months, and the program was nine months long, with occasional exceptions made. A few months before I left Hoisington, I had all kinds of relapse warning signs. I was actually afraid to leave but knew that sooner or later I would have to face life outside of my safe zone. I should have shared these fears with my counselor, but as had happened before, I hurt myself by letting my pride get in the way, and said nothing.

I convinced myself that I could do this on my own, and it was time for me to leave the safety net of the treatment center. I needed to decide where we would live, if I was going to leave my husband or stay and set up a plan of action for my recovery/relapse prevention. The first step was to get a sponsor.

Chapter Twenty-Six

I knew lots of people in recovery, but I still found it hard to reach out to people for help. I remember feeling like I had to hurry up and decide what to do. I convinced myself that staying in Hoisington where I was safe was a copout. The real test would come when I went back to familiar surroundings and everything that I had left to enter treatment.

I had a car by now, and decided that I would return to Topeka where I knew people in recovery. Plus, I'd decided to give my marriage yet another chance. However, I made the stipulation that we would not live together until we were sure that things were going to work out. C.B. did not like the idea of living separately, but I now believe that he only agreed to this to get me to leave Hoisington, where things were really good for the children and me. Sometimes not only addicts, but people in general, do not want to see a person they are involved with change or do better for themselves.

I contacted a friend who was kind of like a surrogate mother to me. I had met her years before in cosmetology school. She and her husband owned rental property and I rented one of their houses, and got everything set up to move in. I especially needed a phone. When you're in recovery, you must have a phone, so you know you can always pick up the damn thing and ask for help.

It was a sad day when I left Hoisington with my boys. I don't know how many times I almost turned that car around to go back. But I also believed it was time to leave and start to put to use some of my tools of recovery I learned there.

As soon as I got to Topeka, I went to WRC, where I had been in treatment before. I saw my counselor there and got set up for their relapse prevention group. WRC had bought an apartment building across the alley from the treatment center. Their offices were on the bottom floor, and the first and second floors were used for apartments for women to rent after treatment if they chose to do so. It was another safe haven for women in recovery.

After arranging for the relapse prevention group, I took the boys to see C.B. at his apartment. He was excited to see us, and we spent some time together as a family that day. I was still wary of him, but he seemed to be happy to see the boys and they warmed up to him pretty well. I had some things to put away at my house, so I left the boys with C.B. for awhile. When I returned to pick them up, a woman friend of my C.B.'s was there. He introduced her and explained that they had met in treatment and she sometimes gave him rides to meetings. I really didn't think anything of it at the time. I myself had several male friends in recovery.

I got myself and Sultan and Malachi settled in our house. I got them into daycare, which S.R.S. paid for. I got a job with the friend I rented the house from, working at her beauty shop. C.B. did not work. Someone along his way had told him that drug addicts could qualify for disability, and he was also claiming dyslexia to help that process along. He was even living rent- and bill-free, due to some program he had signed up for that paid everything and also gave him food stamps. That was a clear sign to me that he was copping out and still into addictive behaviors. When you get clean, you try to turn from using different systems to carry you.

That also told me that even if we stayed together, I could not depend on him for any support. Plus, while I was thinking we were working on our marriage, it turned out that C.B. was in a relationship with the "friend" I met at his apartment the very day I returned.

I realized this by going by late one night to talk to him about some things that I was dealing with. I was actually having some thoughts of using and believed that if I talked to C.B., I could talk my way out of it. When I got there and knocked on the door, it took him so long to answer that I was about to leave. When C.B. finally opened the door, he had a funny look on his face. But this didn't register with me until I walked past him into the apartment. It was a studio apartment, and there on the sofabed was his friend from treatment.

When it hit me what was going on, I wanted to kill C.B., but I was actually proud of my response. I called him a sackful of dirty names and turned around and walked out. It was clear to me in that instant that I had my answer about the divorce. It was also clear that misery loves company. He had begged, made all kinds of promises and cried like a baby for me to come back from Hoisington and not divorce him. But it turned out he only wanted to bring me back down to his level because I was doing so well.

Although C.B. said he only started seeing the other woman because he was lonely after I took his kids and went to Hoisington, after that night my mind was set. I was through with him, once and for all. And my reason for not going out and getting high that night was to show that bastard that I was strong and did not have to get high over his bullshit. For once, hurt and anger saved me from using. I say "hurt" because even though my heart had changed toward him after the incident in Atchison, he was still my husband and the father of Sultan and Malachi. And when I left Hoisington, I left the wreckage from our marriage there. I had returned with a sincere openness and willingness to try and give it an honest chance, only to find out that working things out was never part of C.B.'s plan.

Chapter Twenty-Seven

On my return to Topeka, I tried to go to at least one AA or NA meeting a day. I had reached out and asked a woman in my NA group to be my sponsor, so when I got home that night I called her. I should have called her in the first place, but I was also trying to reach out to my husband. I now believe that it was meant for his infidelity to be revealed as it was, so that I wouldn't have any more doubt about what to do.

My sponsor told me to go back and work the twelve steps and apply them to what was happening in my life now. She told me to go to meetings and talk about my feelings surrounding the situation. I did everything she told me to do. She told me to start and complete my fourth step, which is a searching and fearless moral inventory of myself, I had to go over it with my sponsor, then release it and let it go.

I had planned a trip to see my dad in Illinois. He hadn't seen the boys yet and I wanted to take them by train. My sisters and I had always traveled by train to see him when we were kids and I thought it would be exciting for Sultan and Malachi.

I left my completed self-inventory with my sponsor, with the plan that when I returned, we would burn it or get rid of it however I decided. When I got back, I would also figure out what it would take to get my divorce. But first I needed to take this trip, to get to a place where I could process the fourth step in my mind and just have some peace and serenity after all that had happened.

Our visit with my dad was great, although Sultan got stung by a bee. I think that's the most excited I've ever seen my dad. When he came running back to the house with Sultan screaming, he was so shook up, I didn't know which one to tend to first.

The decision to ride the train there and back was a big mistake. Sultan and Malachi were too young to appreciate the train ride. I would rather have pushed them home in strollers than to get back on the train to go home. But I had the tickets, so we took the return train ride. The saving grace was that they slept all the way back.

The day we got back to Topeka, I was ready to meet with my sponsor. My mind was clear and I had a plan of action where my marriage was concerned. I was still hurt and angry that C.B. didn't just tell me, instead of me having to find out he was cheating on me the way I did. But I now knew that there was nothing wrong with me, and that it was okay to talk about my problems openly and honestly without guilt and shame and without using. Also, during the time back in Topeka, I had built up a pretty good support system, which I now knew was an important part of recovery.

When I called my sponsor that day, I couldn't reach her. C.B. had come by to see the kids and was acting like he had a secret. I put it off as me just being suspicious because of what had happened and let it go.

Later that evening I went to an NA meeting that was held in the basement of a church. I noticed when I got there that C.B. was being dropped off by his treatment friend. I guess she thought she didn't need a meeting. I was excited to be back and to share how well my trip with my boys had gone and how positive I was feeling about my recovery.

At this point I had a little over a year clean. There were a lot of people at the meeting that night. I noticed my sponsor was there and I couldn't wait to tell her about the trip and all the soul searching I had done while I was away. And I was especially excited because I had begun to reach out and put my trust in others like never before. Completing my fourth step and sharing it with her before I left had given me such a sense of relief.

Finishing the fourth step immediately leads you to the fifth step, which states, "Admitted to God, to ourselves, and to another human being the exact nature of our wrongs." That other person should be someone you can completely trust because you share all. This includes things not meant to be shared with everyone, as to do so could cause harm and or injury to others.

The intent of the fifth step is to help the person working it to write it down, accept his or her faults for what they were, share them with their sponsor, pastor or other trusted individual, then let it go. This enables us to move on from the wreckage of our past. That night I felt like I was truly ready to tackle this next step in my recovery.

At some point at the meeting, I got up to go to the restroom. I saw my sponsor and smiled and mouthed, “Hi.” I was about to come out of the restroom when she came in. She looked white as a sheet and scared shitless. I was all excited, ready to tell her about my trip, but she said she really needed to talk to me. My sponsor then proceeded to tell me that while I was gone, she and C.B. had slept together, and she had shared my fourth step with him.

I went from excitement straight to rage. I slapped the shit out of her. I would have bashed her head in, but I was in a church bathroom, and she wasn’t worth it. She had twelve years clean and I had known her for five of those years. I truly thought I could trust her.

She immediately left the meeting and I was so angry that I went back out there and shared with the group what my sponsor had told me. That was wrong. I felt so angry, hurt, and betrayed that I wanted her to hurt too.

The next thing I did was to go home and call her house. Her fiancé answered. He is one of the nicest kindest people I know. I felt like he should be told what happened. I was on a mission from that point on to make sure everyone in recovery and anyone who would listen heard from me what a sorry bitch she was. Even though I never spoke her name while telling the story, everyone who knew me knew that she had been my sponsor. Every meeting I went to, I talked about what happened. I talked about it until it didn’t hurt any more and the anger toward her subsided.

Some would say that it was me taking care of myself. But I knew in my heart that I was being vindictive. I guess there may have been a better way to handle it. And I never meant to hurt her fiancée, who then broke up with her.

I talked about this incident with my former sponsor about six months after it happened. I felt like I had to talk to her about it. I felt so hurt and betrayed in the beginning that all I could feel was rage and vindictiveness. But the more I talked about it at meetings, the more I was able to gain acceptance for what happened and move forward. It was actually a blessing in disguise.

When we talked, she said that she had always been attracted to C.B. What she didn't know until after she slept with him was that he knew I was doing that fourth step with her before I left, and he wanted to know what I had written. I guess he thought that if there was anything about me sleeping with another man while I was with him, then he could justify his infidelity when I had back from Hoisington.

But I was faithful to the marriage to the end. I don't do two men at a time. I never have and I never will. C.B. had used my sponsor for that purpose, even while he continued to see his girlfriend from treatment. So, in the end my sponsor got screwed and C.B. contracted Hepatitis C from her.

Chapter Twenty-Eight

My former sponsor relapsed shortly after her fiancée put her out, and so did my husband and his treatment girlfriend. I lost a sponsor and went right back to not trusting others. I realized that I couldn't trust even myself to make the right choices most of the time. I haven't had just one sponsor since then.

C.B. continued to see the boys on and off. One morning he came by the house while I was getting ready for work. I had the boys dressed and ready to go, and I had just heated up a cup of coffee in the microwave. He started an argument with me because he thought I was seeing someone. I wasn't, but I didn't tell him that. It was none of his business, since I had made it clear that I was through with him.

Malachi was walking around in his walker. I had set my coffee on the television, toward the back, so neither one of the boys could reach it. I was not thinking about the doily on the top of the television that was within reach of the boys.

I was in the bathroom doing my hair, and C.B. was in the living room with them, fussing about whoever it was I was supposed to be seeing. All of a sudden, Malachi screamed. He had pulled the doily and the hot coffee splashed in his face. I grabbed him and ran for the car to take him to the hospital. C.B followed right behind me yelling, "You stupid bitch, you set that there so he would get burned." When we got to the hospital, C.B. told the nurses and doctors that I threw the coffee in Malachi's face on purpose. The doctor finally told him to shut up or he would be asked to leave. He also explained that he could tell by the way the coffee hit Malachi's face that it was not intentional.

I was hysterical and crying, I just knew that my baby was going to be scarred and that it was my fault. I thank God that he was alright. Within a few weeks he was healed with no signs of scarring. But his dear old miserable dad called S.R.S. and they came to my house, because he told them that I was abusing my kids and had burned Malachi with coffee. Here "they" were, back in my life. After checking me out, my house, my children and talking to the doctor in the emergency room, sixty days later S.R.S. left me alone.

I had always said that, no matter what, I would not keep their father from seeing the boys, but after that. I told C.B. that he would have to set up visitation through the court because he really wasn't concerned about Sultan and Malachi at all. He was only trying to get to me.

C.B. threw a glass beer bottle at me out in front of the house that day and split the back of my right leg open. I had to go to the emergency room and get stitches. I still have that ugly scar on my leg. I knew then that I had to stop all communication with C.B. It was almost as if he couldn't stand to see me clean and doing well for myself and the boys. I was becoming independent, where I used to be so co-dependent. To me, that was a sign that I was growing in recovery and I didn't need C.B. and all the chaos he brought into my life.

That's how things appeared on the outside, but on the inside I was a mess. After the incident with Malachi, I started feeling afraid that SRS was going to be hounding me. And I started thinking that maybe I wasn't doing such a good job after all. It takes a lot of self-affirmations for addicts to stay positive. When things start going well for us, for some reason we tend not to believe in ourselves enough to believe that we deserve the good things to happen to us. I know that for me, although I thought the guilt and shame were gone, they were still there. I was constantly beating myself up. I always wanted to do more and be more.

I relapsed again shortly after that. And I also went running back to treatment. I was only allowed into outpatient treatment this time. Treatment had become my safe haven. I did treatment so well that I could have started and run my own treatment center by this time.

What it actually boiled down to is that most times I found myself in relapse because I really didn't believe in myself. It may seem strange, but most people I met who didn't know that I was an addict couldn't believe it when they found out. You should have seen the look on some of their faces when I told my story. Anyway, I went running back to treatment. By the time I finished the program, I had quit my job and didn't have any money.

Fortunately, the apartments across the alley from the treatment center that were being fixed up for women in recovery were ready. The boys and I got to move into the first apartment. I got a job at JC Penney Styling Salon and S.R.S. helped me to get the boys into daycare. I continued to go to meetings and even began to chair the meetings. By this time Cocaine Anonymous (CA) was coming along, and I went to those meetings too. All of the "A's" – AA, NA, CA – are based on the same twelve steps. Although these meetings bring the same message to addicts, some only choose to go to one or the other. No matter what 12- step program you're in, they work if you work them.

I finally had gotten myself back on track, and Sultan, Malachi and I were doing well. We had a nice apartment and my mom had given me a car to get around in. We had our little daily routine down. I was back to chasing Sultan, who was two years old by now, down the alley every morning. We definitely got our exercise. After that, they went to daycare and I went to work. We had breakfast together in the mornings and dinner in the evening. I'd put Sultan and Malachi both to bed at night and by morning they were both in my bed with knees, elbows, and little feet everywhere. I miss that so much.

I didn't actually see my other children very much at this time, but I talked to them over the phone as much as I could. I don't think that my cousin and her husband trusted me enough to let them come visit, but whenever I went to Atchison they never hesitated to let me see them.

I made sure that I got to three meetings a week. Although I was happy with my little family, I began to get lonely. I had lots of male friends but most of them were part of my recovery support system, and not really the types of men that I would be any more than friends with. We all understood that and never even thought about crossing those boundaries. We all had one common goal and that was to stay clean and support each other in doing so. I had several women friends in this support system as well.

Instead of having one sponsor, I used my support system and had many sponsors. After my first and last sponsor I never could bring myself to ask anyone else. I always found a reason why not to ask one person. To this day, I get different views and ideas from each one. I use what I can and leave the rest.

I had told myself that I would stay out of a relationship for awhile. It's highly recommended to avoid getting involved with someone for at least your first year of recovery. I needed to focus on my myself and my recovery and on raising my sons. But I also wanted them to have a male in their lives to do "guy things" with them. One of my friends would come and get the boys from time to time and maybe take them to the park or just come by the apartment and play with them. This allowed me to go to a meeting or just have some time to myself.

Chapter Twenty-Nine

One night after close to a year in recovery, I went to an AA meeting at a treatment center where I had gone for detox several times but, had never actually done treatment. At the meeting, I shared about how lonely I was. I wasn't necessarily looking for a relationship, but just someone to spend some time with like going to the movies, out to dinner, and so on. I was only being honest about how I was feeling. This guy came up to me after the meeting and we talked for awhile. He was in treatment at the center. He told me how beautiful I was and how he'd like to get to know me. I told him that I wasn't looking for a relationship and since he was still in treatment, he should be focusing on his treatment. I could tell from the conversation that he was a very intelligent person, but then most addicts are.

It takes an intelligent person to pull off some of schemes and scams that we as addicts have done. I'm not bragging, nor am I proud of anything I did while on drugs and alcohol. But I have to say, most addicts are very smart people who made bad choices and got hooked. It can happen to anyone; drugs do not discriminate. And absolutely no one can change overnight.

Just because a person enters a substance abuse treatment program doesn't mean they went there to actually get treatment. You will find more people in treatment in the winter than any other time. It's cold out there.

The man I'd just met, Lucifer, wanted my phone number, but I didn't give it to him. I told him that I would call him at the treatment center. We talked on the phone quite a bit and I eventually gave him my number. We talked about the medical profession, which I was hoping to get back into, and Lucifer claimed he was going back to school for after he got out of treatment. He even had me go meet his mother at her house before he got out. She was a very nice Christian woman. She was kind of sickly, but my boys liked her too. She seemed like a good person who had had some problems in her life and had turned to the Lord for her strength. I like to think of her as a prayer warrior.

When Lucifer got out of treatment, he and I, along with Sultan and Malachi, spent a lot of time together. Most of the time we were at his mom's house, where he lived. He couldn't come to my apartment because it had to be approved to have male visitors, and I really wasn't sure that I wanted him there. That was my boys' and my place and I didn't want to share that with him. I had had enough bad experiences with men already, and was afraid to bring anyone in who might interfere with our lives.

After Lucifer had been out of treatment for a little while, I realized there was something about him that bothered me, but I just couldn't put my finger on it. He was very smart and nice, almost too nice. He talked a lot about how smart he was and how he had applied to medical school, and I just didn't believe that at all. It was almost like he was trying to convince me that he was someone he wasn't. I think that his being so nice caused me to overlook or should I say, set aside, my intuition. Plus, Sultan and Malachi seemed to like him, which I considered a real plus.

I soon found out that Lucifer was getting a disability check. This should have been a major warning sign. When I asked about it, he told me some asinine story and I actually believed it. I still wonder why, after all this time, I was still so naïve. I guess I just kept hoping that I had finally found someone who was true. I kept wondering when Lucifer was going to get a job or at least check into school.

We sometimes went to AA, NA or CA meetings together. But Lucifer decided that he really wasn't getting anything out of them, so he quit going. It really didn't bother me at first, because one of the biggest problems before relapse is trying to work another person's program for him or her. No matter how much we want to see someone else do well, they have to want this for themselves to progress in recovery.

Lucifer volunteered to keep the boys one day when I went to work. He said he wanted to spend some time with them. And I really wanted them to be able to interact with other males, not just me all the time. So I said okay, and he was soon spending at least one day a week with Sultan and Malachi. Lucifer didn't have a car, so I would drive to his mom's house with the boys, then he and the boys would drop me off at work.

This went on for about a month, until one day he didn't pick me up. I called everywhere I knew to call. Lucifer's mom and stepdad ended up picking me up. I was so pissed off, I didn't know what to do. By the time we got to his mom's house, Lucifer was there with the boys. My first thought when he didn't pick me up was that he had relapsed, but when I saw him it didn't appear that he had been getting high. He said they had had a flat tire and he had to get it repaired because my spare was no good.

I took the kids back home that night, but something just didn't seem right. And then it came to me that I had met him clean and sober and I would have no idea what he would be like if he did relapse. Up to this point his attitude and behaviors were not of someone using. But since I didn't know what his attitude and behaviors were like when he was using, I couldn't be sure if he was lying or not.

I got out of bed and went down to check my trunk to look at my spare tire. Nothing had been moved around, and nothing was out of place in the trunk. The next morning, I looked at the tire real good and there was nothing wrong with it.

I didn't see or talk to Lucifer much for the next few days. He called to see if I was still upset with him. It was clear that he had lied to me, and I told him that I needed to talk to him about some concerns I had, so I drove to his house. Just as I got there, his ex-wife called him. I told Lucifer that I would leave and talk to him later, but he asked if I would take him by his ex-wife's house. During all this, he just wasn't acting like the person I met. He was anxious and nervous, acting like he just had to get over there, right away.

I felt that Lucifer was trying to avoid my talking to him about him not picking me up from work. I agreed to take him by his ex-wife's house, and on the way, I asked him flat out if he had relapsed. The next thing I knew, I thought my head and eardrum would or had burst. After he hit me, Lucifer yelled, "No one questions me!" He said that just because I'd been clean a year didn't mean that I was better than him. I told him to stop my car and get the hell out and to stay away from my kids and me. Lucifer didn't hit me any more, at least not that day. I dropped him off at his ex-wife's and went home.

Chapter Thirty

Lucifer kept calling for a few days, leaving messages asking me to please forgive him. I didn't call him back. Everything had happened so fast that day, I think I was still in shock that he hit me like that and said what he said. I had never acted as if I was better than anyone and the way he hit me let me know that he was an abusive man; he even looked like a monster that day. I could not believe that someone that nice and intelligent could also be so evil and mean.

Lucifer called again, begging me to talk to him and saying he needed help. One thing about me is, after I got clean, I always felt a need to help others. And of course, I didn't know then that this is what he did with all the women he became involved with. He found out their soft spots, told them everything he knew they wanted to hear, and then he would beat the shit out of them whenever he felt like it.

Lucifer got it back together for awhile and I gave in and started seeing him again on the condition that he get some help for himself. He went back to treatment for thirty days, and went to one anger management group. After being out of treatment for two weeks, Lucifer relapsed again and I had to go to the dope house to get my car so that I could pick up my kids from daycare. By this time, because I was so involved with Lucifer and his issues, I had allowed a lot of my meetings and friendships to fall by the wayside. Looking back, I now know that he made it a point to alienate me from everyone who cared about me and everything I enjoyed doing.

My life was spinning out of control once again. If I told Lucifer that he couldn't use my car while I was at work, he'd beat me up and take it anyway. I didn't feel like there was anything I could do to get away from him. I called the police a few times and they ended up doing nothing. The police would occasionally arrest him on outstanding warrants for other things he had done, like stealing checks or credit cards, but never for beating me. The more I learned about what Lucifer was really like, the more he beat me. In his mind he saw me as better than him and he couldn't stand that.

By this time, I was so afraid of Lucifer and so frustrated at not being able to stop his abusive and controlling behavior that, after over a year's clean time not using, I gave up and started getting high with him. We ended up riding around day in and day out from dope house to dope house with my little boys in the back seat, sitting in their car seats. I don't even know why I still somehow had enough sense to put them in car seats.

Sometimes I would take them to daycare that S.R.S. was still paying for. But with Lucifer now driving all the time, I always picked them up late. If I happened to run into my older sister Aileen or my little brother, who both also lived in Topeka, they wouldn't talk to me or even acknowledge me. Although I was desperate and miserable, I was unable to reach out and ask even my closest relatives for help. Once again, it was that old shame and guilt that made me feel like I deserved no better than I was getting.

Since leaving prison, I had stayed out of legal trouble until getting involved with Lucifer. He had stolen checks and a credit card from some lady. I tried to use the credit card and went to jail and was later charged with theft of a stolen credit card. Lucifer and I took turns going back and forth to jail. Whether it was him or me that was locked up, it was a welcome break for me when we were apart.

I ended up back on probation. I just knew that if something didn't turn around soon, I would be back in prison for those types of petty crimes or for killing Lucifer, because that was the only way I could think of to keep him away from my kids and me. I was so far gone, I couldn't even look into their little eyes anymore. I was so ashamed of what I had become. And I was too afraid to leave, because every time I tried Lucifer would find me. I got put out of my apartment at WRC because I had relapsed and was behind on rent. I went over there and got our clothes and left everything else. Now my children and I were homeless. Lucifer's mom let us stay in her house, where Lucifer still lived. She knew that we were both using, but I think she allowed me and my boys to stay there because she felt that her son was partly to blame for what had happened.

That arrangement was right up his alley. None of my friends in recovery would come around. There was only one that I kept close contact with whenever I was what addicts call, "back out there." I'm thankful to him for being there as a constant in my life, in and out of recovery. I consider him a true friend; he never gave up on me even when I had given up on myself.

We moved into Lucifer's mother's basement and things only got worse. I finally decided I was going to leave, no matter what he said or did. I had had enough, and my boys didn't deserve this life. And who knew how they were being treated when I wasn't around. I took Sultan and Malachi and went to stay with two women I had met in a previous treatment program. They knew the boys and loved them dearly, but I did not want to risk their home or recovery in their willingness to help me to get away from Lucifer. They were two very special people in our lives.

What I failed to realize until the boys and I stayed with these friends for a short time was that other women in the program had admired my strength and determination to get clean and stay clean. They told me that they didn't know anyone who could lose her children and still continue to try and do better. That actually gave me some hope. Here I was, this woman they looked up to and admired, standing here beaten down mentally and physically, looking like death on a stick. How could they admire me?

These kind women took us in and took care of us. I kept a low profile because I knew that if Lucifer found out where I was, he would try to cause them trouble. I started going to meetings again; that's one place where I knew I wouldn't run into Lucifer.

We stayed with my friends for a few weeks and I got a job, and was starting to feel good about myself again. I had everything set up to get another apartment as soon I got my first paycheck. I had decided I would go back to school and I had to get a record of my GED, which I had lost somewhere along the way. The day I got my first check, I went with Sultan, Malachi and one of the women I lived with to cash it and stop and get a copy of my GED. Then we would go and get my new apartment. I was feeling hopeful and positive for the first time in months.

We came out of the building where I had just picked up the copy of my GED, and Lucifer was passing in a car. He jumped out, ran over, hit me and snatched my purse with every dime I had. He jumped back in the car and took off.

Chapter Thirty-One

"Why in the hell wouldn't he leave me alone"? And what was I supposed to do now? Since Lucifer saw me with my friend, he would know where I was staying. I knew I had to leave my friends' home for their own safety. I called the police and made a report, although I correctly assumed they wouldn't follow through. I called Lucifer's mother and told her what had happened. She said she couldn't believe he would do that, but told me to make sure and call the police because he had gone too far this time, She said that, as she was his payee, she would return my money when his disability check arrived. I still needed to find somewhere else to live.

Later that night when I was going into my friends' apartment building with Sultan and Malachi, Lucifer jumped out of the bushes and started beating me. The kids ran into the building screaming, and someone called the police. The women we were staying with came out and started hitting and pulling trying to get him off of me; that's when Lucifer started kicking and stomping me. The police got there. Incredibly, they did not arrest Lucifer. I never understood until later why they always let him go. It turns out that Lucifer was an informant for the sheriff's department. That's how he always found out where I was; someone at that office was telling him. I found this out by calling a pager number he used to call all the time, and a detective called me right back.

The police told me that I should check into a battered women's shelter. This is what I did, even though my friends didn't want me to leave. But I didn't want any more trouble at their house. Once at the shelter with the boys, I got a restraining order (as if that would help). It was only about a week before Lucifer found me there. Since the police took me there, I believe that they are who told him where I was.

The shelter moved the boys and me to another one. Lucifer found that one too. I asked one of my sisters if we could live with her for awhile, but she said she didn't have room. Finally, I just gave up and decided that this was what my life was going to be. I was worthless at everything I tried to do. The police never did a thing, and I had run out of options to keep Lucifer from finding us. I went back to his mother's house with Sultan and Malachi and started getting high with him again. Riding around with the kids in the car picked up where it left off, along with Lucifer's regularly beating me. The awful cycle had started all over again.

I don't know when the last time was that I had looked in the mirror. When I finally did, I saw a broken soul that appeared to be dying a slow death. I remember hoping that death would go ahead and take me out of my misery. I knew that it wouldn't take much more dope or beatings from Lucifer to get the job done. I just wasn't sure which one would prevail in ending my life.

During one of my moments of sanity, I came up with a plan to get my children out of this situation. I couldn't stand for them to go through this any more. I think I also knew in the back of my mind that I could get away from Lucifer more easily by myself. I had talked to S.R.S. a couple of times about my situation, asking for help. All they could offer was to put my boys in foster care until I got myself together.

I wasn't having that after what S.R.S. had put me through over my other children, and their eventually being permanently taken from me. But I was now at a point where I couldn't keep even myself safe. And I was afraid that Lucifer would start in on them. I made my mind up to leave the boys at their daycare, knowing that the provider would eventually call Child Welfare to pick them up when I didn't show. I only prayed that I would be able to eventually get them back. I also prayed that they would forgive me. We were all we had.

Lucifer was very suspicious that day, but most crack smokers are like that most days anyways. We took Sultan and Malachi to daycare. It tore my heart out knowing that I wouldn't be back to get them, but I had to keep them safe and I just couldn't give them what they deserved. I thought that all my insides would rupture and I'd just die from how I felt. But I had to hold it all in, because I didn't want Lucifer to realize what I was doing.

When he realized we were late picking up the boys, Lucifer wanted me to call and tell her we were on our way. We stopped at a pay phone and I pretended to call. When I got off the phone, I told him the daycare provider said she was having a birthday party for one of the other kids and it was okay for them to stay longer. I knew if we went to get more dope, Lucifer would forget about it until later.

When you're getting high, you seem to lose all sense of time. Hours turn into days, days into weeks. It was late the next day before Lucifer even thought about the boys again. When I called this time, I was informed that S.R.S. had picked them up since I hadn't returned, just as I figured would happen.

I wanted to scream, and I did. But I was also relieved, because I knew that the boys were safe. For a very long time, everyone who heard this story thought that I was the most terrible mother on earth for getting so high that I forgot to pick up my kids. No one knew the real reason behind my actions that day until years later.

I thought I was terrible too. And Lucifer beat me over every inch of my body when he found out that S.R.S. had picked them up. I really don't know why he cared. I wasn't getting any financial assistance for them, and he certainly didn't love them like he said he did, but who was I to talk. I felt like I deserved the beating for what I'd done to my own children.

Chapter Thirty-Two

I was nothing more than a walking zombie after that. I couldn't eat, sleep or function at all without drugs. I was nothing but skin and bones. I weighed about ninety-eight pounds, and at age thirty one, I was on a mission of death. I just knew that either Lucifer would kill me or I would kill him. I didn't think about or feel anything but ways to kill him. I blamed Lucifer for my having to give up Sultan and Malachi the way I had. He wouldn't leave me alone. The police were no help and neither was anyone else I asked.

I saw myself as a nothing. All I could think about was my babies and killing Lucifer. I really didn't want or have the desire to get high anymore. But it was the only thing that could suppress the hurt and pain of what I had done to my children. The pain was unbearable. This may sound crazy, but without the drugs, I know that I would have laid down and died. I had no kind of support system anymore. I was too ashamed and so full of guilt that I couldn't have asked anyone for help.

Lucifer used all this to his advantage. Every minute of every day, he reminded me what a worthless, ignorant bitch I was. And if I said anything back, he would beat me. All this time, I never thought about turning to God for help. Lucifer thought for me, talked for me, and made all decisions for me. And I didn't care.

Something happened with Lucifer that finally landed him in jail for some outstanding warrants. I can't remember what they were for, but none of them were for kicking my ass. While he was in jail I was determined to get away, but the shame and addiction to the drugs still kept me from asking for help.

Then something happened that I believe was a message from God telling me not to give up. I was at the drug house getting high. I was feeling relaxed and relieved because Lucifer wasn't around. I ended up selling my car for drugs that night, but I forgot I had sold it. I finally emerged from the house after I was out of dope. My plan was to drive around the corner and get more. When I realized what I'd done, suddenly everything appeared to be outside of myself, as if I were watching a show of my own life. I knew that I had lost everything.

I walked around the corner to get more drugs. As I knocked on the door, the family next door came out to get into their car. They were dressed for church. That's the only way I knew that it was Sunday. The car pulled off, went up the street, turned around and came back. The woman in the car invited me to a women's service that evening at their church. I declined her offer out of fear.

But as messed up as I was, I knew without a doubt that God caused this woman who didn't know me from Eve and saw me knocking on a drug house door, looking like the homeless person that I was, to invite me to her church. At that point I was afraid that, since I had seen what appeared as the filmstrip of my life and then this woman, God was going to punish me. I had gone too far.

No one answered the door at that drug house, thank God. And all the events to that point were weighing on me so badly. I didn't have any money or means of getting any more drugs. That day I made the first positive decision for myself since I'd been back living with Lucifer. I went into detox and later to treatment in Kansas City. While I was gone, Lucifer was released from jail. He started using again right away.

I completed treatment, only because I knew how, after all the programs I'd been through by then. I just wasn't into starting over again and I managed to stay clean for about ninety days. The only thing that kept me going was the possibility of getting Sultan and Malachi back. I made contact with S.R.S. while I was in treatment. I found out that, as when I'd gone through this with my older kids, I needed to find a place to live, a job, attend meetings regularly and accomplish a file cabinet full of other shit to get the boys back with me.

The boys had been split up, because the woman of the family where they were placed didn't want Sultan since, according to her, he was being mean to Malachi. Therefore he was deemed hard to place due to behavioral problems, put on medication, and taken away from his little brother. S.R.S. placed him in a facility, not with a family, even though he was just a toddler, only three years old.

When I got out of treatment, I went into an Oxford House for women. These are homes for recovering substance abusers run by the residents. I was also still in contact with Lucifer, as I feared that if I didn't talk to him there was no telling what he would do. I was deathly afraid of him.

I had regular visits with Sultan, but the woman that had Malachi always came up with excuses. They had Malachi seeing a therapist, and the lady he was living with claimed he was sick whenever I was to visit him. In reality, she was getting too attached. I later learned she hoped to adopt him.

Chapter Thirty-Three

I became president of the Oxford House, and was doing everything I was supposed to do. I was working at a place for severely mentally and physically disabled adults. Part of my job was to transport the clients in the company van to different outings. One night after I dropped off the clients, a priest ran a red light and hit me as I drove through the intersection. My shoulder was thrown out of place, which I believe was due to my wearing a seat belt. But had I not had it on, I may well have been thrown from the van. So thank God for that.

But I couldn't do my job after the car accident. There was a lot of lifting involved in getting the clients prepared for their days. So I was off work collecting workers' comp. At first I tried to get by without medication, but I had to take it because of the pain. This led me into relapse, which started by my taking more medication than was prescribed. This would be my first real understanding of how any mind or mood altering substance can and will lead us back to using.

When I went to treatment before Oxford House, I really did not have another treatment in me. Even when I got to be president of Oxford House and was working and it looked like I was doing so well, I wasn't truly focused on recovery. My focus was only on my children, and I still continued to beat myself up about what I'd done. Oh, how they must have felt betrayed.

If you somehow end up reading this, Sultan and Malachi, I hope and pray that you can find it in your hearts to forgive me. I only wanted what was best for you. I had no help or support from family and I was not the best thing for you at the time. I have lived with my regret from that decision every day that I wake.

I stepped down from the presidency of Oxford House, but continued to attend my meetings for awhile.The pills I had been taking set the wheels of relapse in motion. I just went along for the ride. My first mistake was calling Lucifer, but by then I think I knew that I was going to use anyway. Sure enough, I started getting high again.

When you live in an Oxford House, one of the rules is that if you start using, you have to leave immediately because it puts the other women at risk for relapse. And though I believe that relapse is considered a part of recovery, it shows total disrespect to live in an Oxford House and try to stay there once you have relapsed.

The House is set up for people who are clean and sober. I admitted to the house that I had used. I was voted out, packed my things and left. It wasn't long before I moved back into Lucifer's mother's basement and the beatings started again.

One day we came home and Lucifer's cousin and his wife were there. I knew his cousin from back in school and my own sister used to date his uncle, so we knew each other slightly. I could tell when I first looked at him that he was different. He wasn't drinking or drugging anymore. He and his wife had this aura about them. They invited us both to church and his wife gave me her number to call any time.

This was the second time it became clear to me that God was calling me. Even though I was still using, I really didn't have that drive to do it anymore. I started calling the cousin's wife, and I finally decided to go to church with them, even though my spirit was not with me any more. I had been so wrapped up in relationships and drugs, I never even thought about the existence of myself in a spiritual way.

I was raised in church until about twelve years old, but we were made to go by my grandmother, and I never really paid attention. Plus, Grandma made me think that if I did anything wrong that the Lord would get me, which eventually turned me off on religion.

I had been to church occasionally since then, but never had I seen a church like this. My first thoughts were that I had walked into a cult. It was a Pentecostal church and I remember my grandmother talking about all those people jumping around and speaking in tongues. I was definitely suspicious, but I resisted the urge to just shut them out because of what I'd heard about this kind of church. I now believe this may have saved my life.

All of the people were very nice and welcoming. Most of them were white, which didn't matter to me, but my mind had me thinking that it mattered to them. But the couple I came with was a mixed couple, and they were both clean and sober and happy. I wanted that so bad, I was willing to try anything. The minister gave a good sermon and I met him and his wife after church. I didn't go back for awhile, but I kept in contact with the minister and his wife as well as with Lucifer's cousin's wife.

I know that in the back of my mind I was searching for anything that would help to relieve me of my addiction and my heartache. I had been to treatment eleven times by now, including several times in detox. I thought I had worked the steps to the best of my ability. But my best was clearly not enough.

One day, Lucifer and I woke up after being out for I don't recall how many days of getting high. He was up and ready to get started on our usual mission to get what we began to call our "medication." I didn't want to go. I had been thinking about all the peace and serenity I saw on those people's faces at the church. I hadn't been the same since I went. And Lucifer knew that. I believe he made it his goal to keep me high.

Our normal day consisted of robbing people, stealing or cheating the dope man. Lucifer became angry because I didn't want to go on this mission that day. We fought and fought and I still wouldn't go. I told him that I was tired of getting high and I needed to get myself together. I hadn't even contacted S.R.S. about any visits with my kids because I knew there was no way I would bring them back around him.

I had been with Lucifer for two and a half years, and not many days went by that we weren't high. And not many where Lucifer wasn't beating me up. Any kind of self worth I'd had was totally depleted. I now had a dead spirit. I had gone along because it was all I knew how to do. But whenever I got clean, I became determined, strong and self-assured, which is exactly what Lucifer did not want me to become.

I stayed in the house and didn't use for a couple of days. I tried calling people and praying, but the withdrawal was more than I could stand. My body had to have its drugs. I got high that day and every day until Sunday.

I knew when I got up that Sunday that I had to get to that church. I had to see if Jesus could save me. I was walking death and yet I knew if I could just get clean again, I could be stronger than the drugs.

Chapter Thirty-Four

When I left church that Sunday in 1997, I had been delivered from my addiction, the relationship I was in, and I knew that by God's grace I would never have to use again.

I didn't know where I was supposed to go, though. I had nowhere else to go but back to that house with Lucifer. I prayed for God to lead me. He led me back there. I didn't understand that at all and to this day, I still don't understand that part.

But when I got to the house, I was still excited and I told his mother what had happened. She started shouting, praising God. She apologized for the way her son had treated me. We cried together and she prayed with me. I told her I had to stay there a little longer. This worried her, as it worried me. She and I both knew that she would never tell her son he couldn't live there. She had always blamed herself for his troubles.

I told her I understood what she was thinking but not to worry. I knew that I was in God's hands now. I took my bible, went into the basement and began to study it. I began praying all day every day. The more I focused I became on the word of God, the stronger I got. I soon learned when it was the Lord speaking to me and I was able to discern when it was not of God. Those are gifts I received right off. I also realized right away that my mind was still very much intact and not lost as I had feared. I knew I still had a lot of work to do, but when the Holy Spirit came upon me that day, I knew there was a God who could and would carry me through anything.

Lucifer came home and realized the change immediately. He had the strangest look on his face. I went to the basement and began to pray. Lucifer came down there and asked me if I wanted to get high. I told him that I had been delivered in church on Sunday, and I don't do that any more. He was just staring me in the eyes and I looked straight back at him. I stared him down. He left and stayed gone for two solid weeks.

I knew that the Lord was preparing me to leave there, and I believe he was making sure that I was strong enough and had courage enough. I also knew that no matter what went on around me, He would protect me. I was no longer afraid, and Lucifer knew it. When he came back after those two weeks, he looked at me and said, "You're serious aren't you?" I said, "Yes I am." Lucifer said, "I know you're going to leave me." I told him, "I'm already gone."

He took off again in my car. He just didn't get it. I didn't care about him or things at this point. They were nothing. All I cared about was God's grace and mercy He gave me to get clean. I knew that I would be leaving that house soon. He just hadn't revealed to me how or when. That day came, and had I not been in my right mind, I would have missed my way out. And I almost did.

You see, the "devil," as I choose to call Lucifer now, was only coming by to see if I had given in yet. And I believe that God clearly showing him that I had changed kept him away, even from his own mother's house. He wasn't comfortable in my presence because I was praising God. Everything he stood for had Satan all over it, and he had to flee.

I started talking to my friends in recovery again. I really don't think they believed that I was delivered and visited by the Holy Spirit. But that was one more sign that I had changed. What they thought or believed didn't matter anymore. I knew.

The day that was to be my last in that house, I woke up and somehow knew this would be it. Lucifer's mother and I were sitting on the porch talking and we both seemed to be on edge. That's when the devil came around the corner.

Chapter Thirty-Five

Lucifer pulled up in what I now called "his" car. All I wanted was to be away from him. His mother went into the house. She hated to see him in the state he was in. He called me to come to the car. And just for an instant, I felt that familiar tinge of fear. But it left me as soon as it came. I got into the car and he said, "I know you're going to try to leave me soon." He was smoking dope as he spoke. I remained as calm as I could.

I hadn't been exposed to the drugs since God took the desire from me. I know that God gives us our own free will. We still have the will to take it back or leave it there. Lucifer put more dope on the pipe and tried to hand it to me. I looked him straight in the eye and said, "Satan, flee from me right now! In the name of Jesus!"

I got out of the car, went into the house and called my sister. It was time to go. My sister said she was going to Bingo and running late, but that she would pick me up. I got my bible and some of my things together.

My sister never showed. I was nervous, because I knew that it was time for me to get out of there. When I realized she wasn't coming, I left my things and just took off walking. I knew from the spirit of that encounter with him, that Lucifer would be back. He knew I was leaving. And I knew that, unless he was locked up, I would not be able to leave in peace. But I believed that no matter what or how things happened, God was with me.

I got about halfway up the block and there was Lucifer, waiting in the car. He got out and ran up and kicked me in the ribs. They broke; I felt them snap. I began over and over stating, "Satan flee from me, in the name of Jesus." He pulled me up and hit me in the jaw, also cracking that. I looked in his eyes at that moment and saw nothing but two black holes and an empty shell. I knew that he had no regard for human life. All I was able to get out was, "God help me."

I woke up in the hospital. My ribs hurt so bad I could barely breathe. My face was black. But all I could think of was God and how grateful I was to be alive. And I knew without a doubt that I would never go back there and be treated that way. Not only there, but by any man.

A friend of mine picked me up from the hospital and let me stay with her. She said that I could stay a month. Her husband had gone into treatment. She only had a one-bedroom apartment, and she had a precious little boy.That was the hardest part for me.

This was a true friend. She gave me her bed and slept on the sofa, she clothed me, fed me, and gave me all the support she could. I was helpless for a couple of weeks. I was also afraid of going out because that sicko was stalking the complex trying to find me.

I had nothing by then. I didn't even have any of my own clothes. And I knew I needed to figure out what to do. Treatment had been my escape for so long. But that was no longer an option. I had been delivered, and I had a little over sixty days clean. I needed to come up with a plan.

Chapter Thirty-Six

I started praying. Then I remembered the workers' comp claim I had going from the accident with the priest. I had been so messed up I had forgotten all about it. I called my attorney, who wanted me to hold out for about $25,000. I told him I didn't have time to wait, that I needed to find a place to live. By the end of the week, I had settled for only $1,700. It was just enough to do what I needed to do.

First, I rented an apartment in a locked building. Then a friend I met in recovery sold me an old Chevy Chevette. It was blue with a brown front quarter panel, and had no heat or air, but it ran. I got it at a bargain for $150 cash. Now I needed some furniture. My friends in recovery helped me out in that department. One gave me an old thirteen-inch black and white TV, and another gave a mattress, blankets, and a pillow.

I owed a bill at the phone company, so I bought a "pay as you go" cell phone. That was more for my safety than anything, but since the police never did anything to help, I also purchased a gun, a hot one. No one was going to come between me and my life and recovery.

Lucifer was stalking me like crazy. I did see him a couple of times and told him if he continued to stalk me, I'd stalk back, catch him in an alley alone and blow him away. I was sick and tired of being sick and tired. I also told Lucifer that if he ever came to my apartment, he'd leave with a tag on his toe. He tried to sabotage me, but I just kept right on getting my life together. It took awhile but he finally stopped. I think it took longer for my nervousness to go away.

I got a job with a health care agency and drove back and forth daily to Peabody, Kansas to work sixteen-hour days at a nursing home. I had a two-bedroom apartment, because the plan was for me to reintegrate with Sultan and Malachi. I had a mattress on the floor, my black and white

T.V., and my cell phone and gun and a car and job. But I couldn't remember back to another time when I was that happy and feeling good about myself.

I had been in my new place for nine months when I was about to begin regular visits with Sultan and Malachi. I still didn't even have living room furniture. But I made sure that their room was ready for them to come home.

My visits with Sultan began first and they were supervised ones that took place at Lutheran Social Services. I had been clean nine months when I first saw him again. I also met the woman who, I like to say, saved Sultan's life. When he and Malachi had been split up, little Sultan was placed at Kaw Valley Center in Kansas City, Kansas, and put on God knows what kind of medications to keep him calm.

But God sent Sultan an angel by way of Sharon Kay Greer, a foster grandmother. She was the only one that could get through to him, and she soon took him home as her foster child. When I saw him, he looked and acted like any other little four year-old boy. He was smart as a whip. He knew every make and model of truck on the road. He was loving, outgoing and playful, and most of all, I knew in my heart that he was happy. I met his foster mom Sharon that day, and even though she had never met me before, she said that her goal was to see me and my boys back together and that she and her son were doing all they could to make that happen. They were also trying to get Malachi, so the boys could be together again.

But she also told me about her son and said that he wanted to adopt Sultan and Malachi. I was taken aback by this, and asked about her son. She said he owned and operated his own trucking business. My thoughts were, "Oh no, not an old beady-eyed, pot bellied trucker." Plus, I had no intention of giving up my babies again, to anyone.

S.R.S. and Lutheran Social Services (L.S.S.) claimed that the boys and I would start a reintegration plan, but first we needed to do a time line. This is where you go through your family history to determine where the breakdown in families occurs. They hired an outside contractor to do this. After this, they would decide whether or not to go through with the reintegration process. In other words, my boys' and my future as a family was in the hands of the woman hired to handle my reintegration plan.

It was true that the boys had been in the system for awhile, but I begged S.R.S. and L.S.S. to give me another chance. I did everything that S.R.S. put before me, and was honest in saying that I wasn't quite ready to have the boys return home right then, but that by the time I finished jumping through all of their hoops, I would be ready.

Being honest was the worst thing I could have done. Once I had fulfilled all of the S.R.S. and L.S.S. requirements, I had a year and a half clean. I still had my place and my job and was ready for the boys to come home. But L.S.S. and S.R.S. decided that because of the final report on the time line, I would not get the chance to reintegrate. In other words, the boys would be permanently taken away from me. I was devastated.

My worker at L.S.S. told me that I could continue visits until we went to court. She also informed me that Sultan had become attached to his foster mom's son, Robert, the truck driver. S.R.S. was working on getting Malachi there and Robert wanted to adopt them both. My case worker wanted me to meet Robert with Sultan there to see how they interacted with each other.

When I saw the two of them together, I knew that Sultan had found the father he had never had. Malachi was on this visit as well, and he took right to Robert too. Robert certainly didn't look like the beady-eyed trucker that I had imagined. He was very clean cut, good- looking and businesslike. I had to admit that I was attracted to him. And I could tell that he was attracted to me as well. S.R.S. and L.S.S. encouraged us to spend some time around each other so that I could get to know him and how he did with the boys.

Before Malachi went to live with Robert and his mother, he was still with the family that didn't want Sultan. That woman treated Malachi like a little baby. He whined a lot and hung onto her. And he was calling her Mama. I had a visit with Malachi at his therapist's office and he ignored me through the whole visit. I remember sitting there crying, thinking that my baby didn't know who I was. His foster mom was in the waiting area. When we came out, he ran to her and she picked him up. She was always carrying him around, even though he was three years old.

Malachi just kept staring at me. I knew that I had lost him. And I couldn't stand that woman holding him rocking him, almost making him not want to be around me. After the visit was over, I told the therapist that if we had to visit there that the foster mother would have to drop him off and leave. It wasn't fair to our visit for her to be there.

I was almost to the car when I turned around to tell Malachi goodbye and that I would see him on our next visit. I was crying so hard I couldn't see straight. But I'd be damned if I was going to give up this time. All of a sudden, I heard him crying "Mommy, Mommy!" He jumped down and ran to me and hugged me crying, "Don't leave me." It took everything I had not to jump in my car and leave with him and just get as far away as I could. But I was trying to do things right this time.

Believe me, there will never be a test as great as this one for my recovery to endure. Using was no longer an option for me. I finally wanted to be clean more than I needed to get high. I knew that I would deal with and work through this with God's help and my recovery support.

Chapter Thirty-Seven

Malachi finally got reunited with his big brother Sultan. We continued our visits, only now they were with Robert, who now was both boys' foster father. About six months after Malachi moved in with Robert and his mother, L.S.S. informed me that they, along with S.R.S., would be petitioning the court to terminate my parental rights. If I voluntarily relinquished my rights, then the boys would be adopted by Robert. But if I fought for the boys and lost, and the court terminated my rights, then I would have no say in where they ended up.

For me, it was a Catch 22. I would likely lose the boys either way. I had to take an honest look at my sons and what was going to be best for them. I had never seen them so happy and settled in their lives. I had a year and a half clean, but I'm an addict. I could not gamble their future on whether or not I would use again. And I was scared to death to get them back and screw up again. They deserved every bit of the love and stability they were getting, and I knew in my heart that they were genuinely happy. That's what mattered most to me, was their happiness.

Robert assured me that I would always be able to see the boys whenever I wanted to. He even told S.R.S. and L.S.S. that he would never keep them from me. So, instead of trying to beat the termination, I relinquished my parental rights based on my children's happiness and the promises from S.R.S. and L.S.S., that no one else would be able to adopt them.

I will never forget the day I signed those papers. For the next week or so, I was in a daze. I asked myself I don't know how many times if I done the right thing. They were in Kansas City, Kansas and I was in Topeka. I called every chance I got. I visited them, and they visited me.

By this time Robert and I had begun seeing each other. The more time we spent together, the closer we became. Robert is a truly good and caring man , and is the complete opposite of any man I had ever been with before. We both like to think that it was Sultan who brought us together.

Robert kept having to do more home studies for L.S.S. and S.R.S. before they would complete the adoption process. I began to feel like something was wrong. Then Robert's mother Sharon (Sultan's "angel") became sick with cancer and some woman started writing letters to L.S.S. and S.R.S., saying that Sharon was sick and that the boys were being cared for by unauthorized persons. This was untrue, as the boys were always under the care of Sharon or Robert.

Suddenly, without investigation or warning, S.R.S. came three days after Christmas and removed my children from their home. I had just spent my first Christmas day with them in two years. When Robert called me with the news on December 28th, 1998. I just slid down the wall. I thought I would die.

Robert told me not to worry, that he would do whatever it took to get Sultan and Malachi back. He hired an attorney to try to find out what in hell happened and get the boys returned to him. S.R.S. and L.L.S. wouldn't tell me or him anything. Two attorneys ended up getting paid a lot, but produced nothing. We gave them thousands of dollars until we both ran out of money, and never learned anything.

I haven't seen my boys since. I got so angry that I was on a mission to make as much money as I could so that if I ever saw them anywhere I could snatch them and run if I had to. People who I'd thought were my friends bullshitted me along the way. Some would say that they knew where the boys were, even though they didn't know a thing. I don't think they realized what raising these false hopes did to me.

Some of my old attitudes and behaviors returned, and I began to not like myself again. I got a job part-time at a mental health center and I think that they helped me more than I helped them. Although I was angry with God, I still prayed and claimed deliverance from my addiction. I was determined not to use. Using had taken everything from me, and I was too damn angry to go back to that.

Thank God, for once in my life, anger worked in my favor. I attended meetings and processed my feelings. I talked about it until I was tired of hearing myself talk about it, until the pain wasn't quite as raw anymore, and I didn't want to kill everyone. My prayers became sincere again and I began to focus on what to do with whatever was left of my life. I thought about going back to school, but talked myself out of it several times. I didn't think I was smart enough and I absolutely hate to start things I can't finish and see through to the end.

I'd go to the duck pond a lot and just sit there and cry. I never fed the ducks any more because that was something that Sultan, and Malachi and I always did together, and it didn't seem right without them. We'd save our leftover or crusts of bread or sometimes buy a loaf and every week we'd feed the ducks.

After two years' worth of brush-offs and bullshit by S.R.S., Robert and I were both broke. That was seven years ago; seven years since I've seen my sons or had any idea where they were. Everyone thought that I wouldn't get through this, and I didn't either.

I don't think that S.R.S. ever had any intention of allowing Robert to adopt my boys. I believe in my heart that they wanted me to see them as happy and content as they were, to sway me to relinquish my rights to them, then they could do as they pleased. This was the worst and final betrayal by L.S.S. and S.R.S. I couldn't appeal a relinquishment but I could have appealed a termination. And they didn't have to, nor did they tell me, shit, no explanation at all.

My first reaction was rage. I wanted to go to S.R.S. and dangle all the social workers out the top floor window, and if they didn't tell me where my boys were, I'd drop them. Then I wanted to find out where they lived, take their kids, so they could feel what I was feeling. I was angry at everyone, including God. Why did He deliver me from drugs, then take my children again?

I think about Sultan and Malachi every day of my life. I wonder what they look and smell like. They turned ten and eleven this year. I hope they are happy and loved and have no worries in the world. I pray to God that they are being raised in a Christian home. I love them and miss them so much, that some days I wonder what's the point in getting up. But the point is that whenever we find each other, and I have faith we will, I'll be here to receive them. Clean and sober.

Chapter Thirty-Eight

I was looking through the newspaper one day and saw an ad for a surgical technician class. I certainly needed something a little more exciting in my life. Working as a CNA at nursing homes and as a mental health tech part-time was, I believe, keeping my spirits down. I prayed and asked God to let His will be done. I would have to quit my job to do the training program, which included both in-hospital training as well as classes in Human Anatomy and Physiology.

Robert, with whom I had been in a committed relationship for over two years by now, agreed that if I really wanted to do this, he would pay my rent and bills so that I could concentrate fully on school instead of working part-time. I applied, and a couple of weeks later, I received a letter saying that I was not accepted. It was a let down, but I was okay with it. In fact, I was actually somewhat relieved, because I just didn't believe I had what it took to do the work. I was really afraid that due to my drug use, I wouldn't be able to retain anything.

My prayers were answered. The following week, I was called by one of the nurses who had interviewed me for the class. She told me that one of the other applicants had decided not to take the class and that I was their first pick for alternate. I was so excited that I started crying. I was so happy that I was being given a chance to better myself. Robert came to Topeka and took me shopping for new clothes. I just couldn't believe that things were finally coming together for me.

School was hard for me, and I think that at my age I had to study longer and harder than everyone else. But I made it. Within six months, I was a surgical technologist, scrubbing surgical cases at a hospital.

I am so glad that I applied to that class. It was truly a turning point for me. I love my work. And you have to love it to do it well. Once I realized that I could do as well as my peers at work, my only concern was getting to know other people from different backgrounds. Would they accept me? And what would they think of me, if they knew the person I used to be? For a long time I carefully chose who I shared my past with. Today it doesn't matter. I'm a recovering addict and alcoholic. What I went through was horrific, but it made me much stronger.

I wasn't born with a silver spoon in my mouth and I didn't turn out to be a very good mother, but God forgave me and gave me the courage, strength, and determination to forgive myself. He's brought me back together with my four oldest children. Sultan and Malachi have yet to return, but I believe in my heart that they're coming too.

Chapter Thirty-Nine

My friend Tommy has been a constant support for me since my very first AA meeting after leaving Menninger's. He went through this whole roller coaster ride with me. We've laughed together and we've shared some losses together. Some of those losses were friends in recovery and some who left recovery to try drugs again and never made it back. Tommy was always there waiting for me to come back in after my relapses, never judging, but always curious as to what I would do each time to keep myself clean. He could probably tell my story as well as I can. He's practically lived through it along with me.

Tommy and I shared an experience together that could have ended very badly. We went on what we call in recovery a "13th step" one night to help another person in our support system who had relapsed. We decided that she had too much to lose and we just couldn't let her go without trying to intervene. We found ourselves on the steps of her apartment building, sweating and out of breath, not knowing if we wanted to get her out or join her. You have to know what you're doing when you, as a recovering addict who is fighting relapse yourself, head in somewhere where there's using going on. We ended up realizing that we needed to leave to save each other.

Today the person we tried to rescue is doing great things with her life. But it has nothing to do with us going over there. Sometimes we just have to "let go and let God" fix it. And this was certainly one of those times. We all laugh about that night now, and I'm just glad we can.

Although I was in and out of recovery through the years, I took great comfort in knowing that Tommy would be there whenever I would drag myself back through the door. Since I first met him, no matter what's going on or where we are in our lives, he has always made time to listen to whatever it is I'm going through. That's what I consider a true friend; to know all your deepest secrets and fears and still accept you as you are. Tommy knew firsthand how hard I tried to be a good mother to Sultan and Malachi once I got clean. And he also knew how important their happiness was and still is to me.

Chapter Fourty

While in school, I met another man, Russell, who also became a very dear friend. I met him through a friend of mine who he was dating at the time, but I had already heard about him through his sister and two nieces. I finally met him at an AA meeting. By this time, I had close to three years clean.

Russell became one of the best friends I ever had in my life. I was going through some difficult times in my relationship with Robert, and he was also having some trouble with his girlfriend. We would sit at my house and drink coffee and talk about what was going on with each of us. His situation with his children was similar to mine. We'd talk about our kids and share our dreams about the relationships we would like to have with them. By the time we met one another's families we felt like we already knew them.

Russell and I spent many days and nights talking, and even crying, about our struggles in recovery. I could talk to him about anything and he never put me down or made me feel bad for the way I felt. A lot of people thought that we were in a relationship, and we were, but it was not a sexual relationship. We decided early on that we would remain in a platonic relationship, because neither one of us had ever had a friendship like ours. We loved each other in a way that what we call a "normal" person, who has not been through the struggles of addiction and recovery, could never understand.

The main thing we had in common was that we had both lived alcohol- and drug- addicted lives, which had a direct affect on our lives and relationships with our children, although in different ways. We shared our hopes and our fears about how things would be as our relationships with our children grew. We were a constant support for each other even when we weren't around each other.

My job was going well, but I began to feel that I wouldn't be able to reach my highest potential at my place of employment. The male students from my class who still worked at the hospital seemed to be put on the most challenging cases. I felt that I was being held back, and I was growing restless for a position where I would be given the level of challenge I knew I could handle. I applied to a surgical staffing agency in Kansas City and got hired. I drove back and forth for a couple months, then made the difficult decision to move to Kansas City. I was tired of the drive and I also wanted to be closer to Robert, who was there.

Although I didn't want to leave my house in Topeka and my support system, I saw the move and new job as a whole new beginning. However, the first year was horrible. All I did was work and spend time with Robert and his family. Don't get me wrong, I love them all. It's just that I had no life of my own. And my family wasn't quite together yet. My sisters and I hadn't quite formed relationships with each other like we have now. My recovery support system was back in Topeka, and my phone bills were higher than my rent. And I missed my friend Russell and the times that we had shared.

Sadly, Russell and I didn't keep in touch like we promised we would. I would see him briefly whenever I visited Topeka, but he was in a new relationship with someone who turned out to be an evil jealous woman who would never have understood our friendship. The rare times I did see him, Russell was complaining of back pain that he thought was due to an old injury. I told him to make an appointment with the doctor to make sure that's what it was. He said he didn't have health insurance at his job and he couldn't afford to go. I told him that his health was more important than the worry of having a bill to pay.

Six to nine months passed and Russell still hadn't gone to the doctor, but was relying on someone else's pain medication for relief from the pain. That's like playing Russian Roullette when you're in recovery. As I myself had learned the hard way, pain pills could lead you back to your drug of choice.

The worst part is that another person in recovery was the one giving him the pills. I asked her on several occasions to promise me that she wouldn't give him any more and she told me that she wouldn't. She was a very good friend of mine at the time and I trusted that she would keep her word. We used to be really close and it was a slap in the face to find out she was still doing it. Maybe, just maybe, if she had told him no, he would have gone to the doctor. But most of us aren't very good at taking care of ourselves.

She and I had had our differences and had still maintained our friendship, but this one hit too close to someone that I cared a whole lot about, and I thought she did too. You stick around people long enough and no matter who or what they claim to be, it all comes out in the things that they do. Another friend of ours always said, "If you hang around the barbershop long enough, eventually you're going to get your hair cut." She and I are still able to be cordial towards one another but that's about it.

In 2002, Russell's dad passed away. By this time he had married the woman he starting dating when I moved to Kansas City. She wasn't supportive of him in anything he did. And she didn't want either of them to be around his family. He knew early on that he had made a mistake in marrying her. But being the good-hearted person he was, he tried to make things work out.

During this period, Russell's sister Debbie and I became closer and began to form a real friendship. The more possessive his wife became, the closer his sister and I became, out of shared concern for him. She would always let me know how he was doing. Debbie and I became the best of friends. She now has eleven years clean and continues to be a great support to me and my recovery.

A year after Russell's and Debbie's father died, their mother passed on as well. This was devastating to them and all who knew them. I offered my support and helped out where I could. This was a family that I had grown to love and care about like my own. If I could have taken some of the pain that they had to endure, I would have. But the attack on this dear family did not end there. Early the following year, we learned that the back pain that Russell had been having was cancer in its final stages. The doctor said

Russell had two to three months to live. But God saw it a little differently; he was with us for six months from the time he found out.

The hell that Russell went through with his wife during his struggle with cancer was a terrible thing to see. If I could have taken him away to a secret place and taken care of him in peace, I would have. "Till death do us part" meant nothing to Russell's wife. She soon grew tired of caring for him, and he eventually moved in with Debbie.

I went to see Russell as often as I could. In all his pain, a pain that you nor I could not possibly imagine, he needed to know that God had forgiven him for leaving his wife and home. Even with her unwillingness to give him the care he needed, he felt that he should have stayed at home because that was his duty as a husband.

June 18th, 2004, which was a Friday, would be the last weekend that I would spend with my dear friend Russell. He passed away that Sunday morning, Father's Day. A part of me went with him, but he left me so many great memories. I'm just grateful that I could be there with Russell to try and help comfort him in his last days. His wife to whom he was faithful until death never even showed her face those final days. I think of him always and find comfort in knowing that he had accepted Jesus into his life, and that he died with dignity and respect, surrounded by those who loved and cared for him most.

Chapter Forty-One

When I moved to Kansas City and got settled, I decided that I would help my older sister Aileen get herself together. She had an issue with drug addiction as well. I cannot tell you her story, only the parts she played in mine. I went back to Topeka and got her.

But in my desire to help, I once again lost sight of who I was. All I focused on was helping my sister to get clean and stay clean. When I got clean I wanted everyone I knew to be clean too. Only I was the one doing all the work. In my mission to save her from herself, I had become an enabler. As an addict, I should have known better than anyone that you cannot help anyone unless they want help. I only wanted Aileen to have the peace and serenity that comes with being clean and sober. She obviously was not ready to stop using yet, and in my quest to help her I only enabled her to use more.

One of my nieces came to live with me to complete high school. She had been expelled from school in Atchison with her senior year to finish. My sister Eve asked if she could enroll her in Kansas City, would I be willing to let her stay with me? My response was, "Of course she will stay with me." This was a new experience for me since I hadn't raised my own children. But I still felt that it was my responsibility to help anyone I could, and especially my own family. My niece lived with me for her senior year, graduated, and eventually got a job and her own place.

I was happy about being able to help her, but always felt guilty because I wasn't there for my own children. Don't get me wrong, I wanted to be there. But when your children have been adopted by another family, even if it is a family member, you can only be there as much as they allow you to. I had contact with my children throughout their childhoods. I talked to my children on the phone on a regular basis, and visited when their adoptive parents let me. While I was using I was too ashamed to visit or even call, but even when I was clean, for a long time my cousin and her husband did not trust me enough to allow my children to spend a lot of time with me. And I think for awhile there was the "I'm the parent" struggle. Sure, I was the birth mother, but they were the ones who raised them and took care of them when I couldn't.

We've gotten past that now. About five years ago, I raised the issue of their spending time in my home. I explained that I didn't have to prove anything to them any longer. I had turned my life around, and they were the ones living in my past. I would no longer allow them to use the guilt and shame from my past to control me. If they still couldn't trust me with my children after all this time, I was through trying to get them to. Though it would be extremely painful, I would bow out until my children became of age and could make their own decision about whether or not to have me in their lives.

About a month after this, we started communicating on a much more positive basis, and they began trusting me for the first time. Now I spend time with my children at their home and at mine, and their adoptive parents and I share in the joy and pain of our children.

By the time Eve's daughter graduated and moved out, I had about four years clean. My sister Aileen was again living back at my place along with her daughter, Brenda. We were all adults, but I was the only one in the house working. The money just wasn't enough. So it turned into me taking care of them and my boyfriend, Robert, taking care of me and everything else that I couldn't cover. This went on for about a year, until they continued to disrespect the rules of my house. They moved out and I finally had my house back to myself, along with all the bills they helped to run up.

I like to think they were grateful to me for giving them a place to stay, but I'm not sure. I've never heard it from them. My sister started using again and my niece wanted to run in and out all hours of the night, so she eventually moved out with her mom. I had been going to Atchison pretty regularly to see my four kids and to check on Winsome's grandmother

(her dad's mother). She had severe lung disease and she was also addicted to crack cocaine. I was helping to pay for her medication and was trying to be supportive of her getting off drugs. Little did I know she had been using all the time I had been going down there.

I went to Atchison one evening to get some money that her son, Winsome's uncle, had promised to pay me back for a phone bill I had paid for her so it wouldn't be cut off, as she was so sick. We were sitting there talking and all of a sudden, the police kicked in the door. All of those years that I spent in drug houses and used drugs, and I had never been caught in a raid. And I was one month away from having six years clean.

To top it off, I was the one charged with possession and illegal transport of drugs. This gets better; I was arrested and taken to jail and placed under a $50,000 bond. This was clearly a case of my past coming back to haunt me.

I now believe this was God's way of telling me to stay away from her. And because of my prior history in this town, police and the district attorney actually thought they had a case against me. I hadn't been in the Atchison court system since the 1980's, and they had no idea that I was not the person I used to be. But they soon found out. The real kicker is, the police never could produce any evidence. I had been arrested based purely on my long-ago history in this town.

Despite my innocence, I had to pay an attorney, plus $3500 to get out of jail. When all was said and done, the case was dismissed and I didn't even get an apology. Not to mention the humiliation I had to face on my job when my co-workers at the hospital where I'd now worked as a surgical technician for three years learned I was in jail on drug charges.

There was one positive result out of the whole deal. This was the wonderful letters that my co-workers wrote on my behalf to the court, stating how they knew and viewed the person they worked with. In reading what they wrote about how responsible an employee I was, and that surely they had the wrong person, and that I was an asset to the surgical team and a very important part of that team, a light bulb also came on for me. I knew that I wasn't that person I'd been all those years back in Atchison any more.

Although I had been clean all that time, still in the back of my mind, I never saw myself as doing so well and living such a completely different life as described by those who only knew me since I left that life behind. I saw this as a blessing from God, because even though I was living it I hadn't really seen it or believed it.

Chapter Forty Two

With trying to take care of everyone else and having to pay all that money to get released from jail, which Robert busted his ass out on the road to help pay, I became financially bankrupt. I literally had to file a Chapter 13 Bankruptcy, on top of having had to file a Chapter 7 a few years back after getting clean. I was angry and resentful towards everyone who I had helped and who in turn they either couldn't or wouldn't help me.

Shortly after all this, Brenda, my now twenty-one year old niece, began to get into trouble with the law on a regular basis. She wasn't using drugs, but she dated drug dealers. Her situation growing up was similar to that of my own children, only she never found a real connection with a family who loved her and wasn't just taking her on as a foster child for the money. Therefore she was moved around quite a bit and missed out on having a family who loved and cared about her. Brenda's younger sister went to live with her father, but since only she was his child, he wouldn't take Brenda too. She and her little sister were very close, and I believe the effects of that split only caused her to feel more unwanted and unloved. Because of the physical and mental abuse, that she suffered in and out of different foster homes, I believe she feels unworthy and looks for love anywhere she can get it but has no idea how to receive it. She also has low self-esteem and doesn't feel that anything she does is right.

Brenda's cycle through jails was so similar to my own that I would have done almost anything to help her break that downward spiral. I wanted to believe that if she knew that someone was there for her and loved and cared about her, she would turn her life around and start to do better. Every few months she'd go to jail, and I'd run and get her out again, knowing I couldn't afford it. I was only hoping to save her from the miserable life into which she was running head first. When Brenda got out of jail, she would do the same destructive things over and over, expecting different results each time. Sound familiar?

I knew that I needed to let go and stop trying to save her, but at the same time I knew that that everyone else in her life had given up on her all along the way. I was working my ass off and was behind on every bill I had, including my rent.

Then Brenda called me one day and asked if she could come back and stay for awhile. My first response was no. But after she told me she was pregnant, I changed my mind. Though I hardly had two nickels to rub together, I couldn't leave her with nowhere to go while she was pregnant. This would give us close to nine months. I figured that I could finally encourage her to do better for herself, now that she was about to become a mother.

After Brenda moved back in, I thought things were going well between us. We did a lot of talking, and she shared a lot of things with me that I thought would help her by being able to talk about them without shame. I told her about my giving birth to Blake and having to leave him to go to prison only weeks later. And how upsetting it was that he and I weren't able to bond as mother and son because of that.

I begged Brenda to tell me the truth about all her fines and court appearances. This was her chance to do all those things that she needed to take care of, while she was living with me and carrying her baby. Then she wouldn't have to leave her baby the way that I did during this most important time in both of their lives as mother and child. I would have gone even further into debt to ensure that everything was taken care of, for the sake of her and her bonding with her baby.

Brenda promised me that everything was fine. Then, a few weeks after her sweet baby boy was born, the police knocked on my door. Sure enough, Brenda ended up going to jail for all those things she assured me that she had taken care of. Seeing the look on her face, and knowing that she had lied to me over and over, and realizing what this innocent baby was about to go through made me sick to my stomach. I cannot explain or ever forget her look, although it seemed to be one of disbelief. As I had tried to warn her over and over, the court systems do not care that you're a new mother, you have to be accountable for your actions.

In the midst of all the pain and confusion, my sister Aileen, who I had thought was lost to her addiction, stepped up to the plate, left the drugs alone, and took on the care of her new grandson. This is one of the most profound acts of grace the Lord has shown me.

My sister moved back in with me, and I still struggled financially, but we made it. Every time I touched and held and smelled that little boy, I thought of my own babies. I realized that if I became too attached to him, I would never be able to see him leave me. But we loved him up daily.

Brenda got out of jail four months later after I bonded her out, spending my whole paycheck. I justified this as the baby needing his mother, which he did. While she had been pregnant with him, I had wanted to believe that Brenda and I had gotten closer. I grew to love her as my own child. In my heart I still feel that way and worry about her all the time. But I'm not sure if she's capable of loving or accepting love. When she returned to court she was sentenced to more time in jail. My own earlier life flashed before my eyes.

My sister had started to look for a place for them to live. The week before they were to move, my place caught on fire. I live in a split-level duplex and the fire actually started next door in the neighbor's garage, but my bathroom and one of the bedrooms burned, the one with all of the baby's clothes and other things. I was the one who had purchased everything before he was born. And I didn't have renters' insurance. The Red Cross gave me some cash assistance and I used that to replace most of his things.

My sister and the baby moved into their new place. Brenda was still in jail but was soon to be released. Once out again, she moved in with her mother and her baby. I stayed at Robert's until my place was livable again.

Aileen didn't even offer me to come stay with them. My feelings were really hurt. In addition to everything I'd done for Aileen and Brenda, I gave my sister whatever I could salvage so she would have something to get started in her new place. When you are clean and sober, it hurts to see people for what they really are, and it makes me sad. I can no longer hide from reality as I did when I was using.

But one thing I am is a survivor. I've been starting over all my life. I stayed at Robert's house for four months until my place was ready. I was hoping to get back in before Christmas and I did. Since I moved to Kansas City, my mom, my dad, my sisters, and their children spend most holidays, including Christmas, at my house. My four older children spend Christmas Eve and Christmas morning with their adopted family. But we all get to see my children, usually later Christmas Day, and pretty regularly up until the New Year when it's time for them to go back to school. Sadly, my little brother Christopher never comes around. He's on crystal meth, the drug of his generation and in and out of jail a lot. I believe the shame keeps him away more than anything.

My dad has always come to Kansas for the Christmas holiday, and makes sure to visit all of his daughters while he's here. We used to see him more often when we were younger, but as he gets older he travels less. We all try to be at the same place on New Year's Eve to bring in the New Year together as a family.

When I see my mother and father and all my sisters gathered in one place, I believe that we have truly been blessed as a family. We were torn apart by divorce so many years ago, only to be brought back together by God's Grace and mercy.

Chapter Forty-Three

My mother, who has been a fairly regular churchgoer for years, had started attending her church in Atchison again. They were having Family Day, and she invited me and my sisters to come. Although I had a spiritual relationship with God, I hadn't been to church much since leaving Topeka and hadn't attended regularly even while I lived there. I kept saying I needed to find a church home in Kansas City, but never really made the effort to do so. I really didn't feel comfortable in a church worshiping with others; I just never felt like people were sincere. But all that changed when I realized that I was the one that needed to be sincere about my worship and not focus on anyone else's worship, only my own. It's about my own personal relationship with God.

I accepted my mother's invitation. Most members of my mother's family, the Boldridge's, have been members of Campbell Chapel at one time or another. My grandparents were lifelong members. That day, I felt like I had been going there all along. The pastor and his wife were so welcoming, not overbearing, and down to earth, I couldn't believe it. When I returned the following week, I knew in my heart that I would make Campbell Chapel my church home.

I joined the church, rededicated my life to Jesus, and have been an active member of the church since. I am an usher, a missionary, and I am also the children's Sunday School teacher. My life has been changed profoundly since then. All of my sisters and nieces have joined and try to attend regularly. After so many years of being distant and having little involvement with my sisters and their children, I now have a relationship with each one of them on an individual basis. I believe this is solely the work of God in our lives.

Chapter Forty-Four

My dear friend Debbie, Russell's sister, works for prevention and recovery services. In July of 2004 she asked me to be on a panel for a "town hall" meeting for voices of recovery. I had told my story several times over the years, usually only at AA or NA meetings. Sharing my story with people who don't know what it's like to be an addict is totally different. Although we work at letting go of the shame from our past, it tends to rear its ugly head at times and holds us back.

I agreed to speak. I remember being afraid of how the people there would react. As I looked around the room, I saw some of the people crying, and I started crying too. I talked about what it was like for me as an addict.

I believe that this is the night that I began to let go of all the bitterness and anger toward myself and it really hit me that I had a story to tell that could help others. Almost every time I speak about my past, I cry. I used to cry because it was so painful to talk about what happened with my children, but now there's joy that the Lord has brought into my life mixed in with the pain. Each time I tell my story the pain lessens. I share my story today with whoever will listen, because I believe that God brought me though this life, a life that should have killed me, for me to share it.

A few weeks after the town hall meeting, I was asked to speak at a dinner in Topeka to present a new program for drug-endangered children to the public. I agreed, not knowing who would be present. When I arrived, I was nervous once I realized who all was at the dinner. A woman from Child Protective Services was there, who was very familiar with my case with Sultan and Malachi. The judge who would have terminated my parental rights, had I not relinquished them was present. The sheriff, people from the Kansas Bureau of Investigation, and several others I had come into contact with over the course of my addiction were all there. They were in the dark as well, because the program did not list me by name, but just as "A Mother Speaks Out." They had no idea it was me, the former addict they all remembered, until I introduced myself when I came forward to speak.

And speak I did. About how a system that was set up to keep families together, only helped to tear mine apart. I shared my life-changing experiences as well as the bitterness and anger with the system of S.R.S. I spoke about my anger with the sheriff's department for not keeping the asshole that was abusing me in jail and off the streets, a man who is probably out there abusing some other woman as I speak.

I needed for them to hear from my own mouth what it was like for me, with absolutely no support whatsoever from systems that were set up to help parents and children. Somewhere down the road, the parents were left out and someone forgot that we all didn't come from the same lifestyles and we all didn't make the same choices. I told them, "One thing is true: I am a human being, just like you! And I deserved to be treated as such." I described how my case went from worker to worker, and no one ever followed through to the end.

When I finished, you could have used a shovel to pick the mouths up off the floor. Some had tears in their eyes; they could not believe that it was actually me standing before them alive and very much well, with seven years of recovery, telling them like it was for me. And I couldn't believe it either. When I left my house for Topeka that night, I had no idea what would take place, but I felt strongly that God was with me and he placed everyone there that needed to be there, to see me and hear what I had to say. I think that some of them actually thought that after what happened with my boys, I would just go away, smoke myself to death or just lay down and die.

I had nothing to fear from any of these people anymore; I no longer had anything or anyone for them to take from me. I had come to another turning point in my life that night, and I felt that God still had more work for me to do. The woman from Child Protective Services agreed that somewhere along the way, the ball had been dropped in my case. She told me that she was sorry and only wished she could change the way things had happened. The judge had tears in his eyes and hugged me, and said, "I cannot believe that you are the same person that was in my courtroom all those years ago." The Sheriff invited me to stop by and have coffee or just to visit.

Somewhere during my talk, I believe that God removed the bitterness and anger from me that had been keeping me from moving forward and sharing my story like I should be. Although I don't fully trust their word, I have forgiven these people in my heart, which has only helped to restore my soul to sanity.

More blessings were on the way. Shortly after that evening, I was contacted by a woman who also works for S.R.S. She wanted to meet with me to talk about a new program that they are getting off the ground, called Systems of Care. She also offered me a seat on the statewide steering committee for the new program. There was something about her that I liked immediately, but in my mind I was warning myself, "Remember who she works for."

When we did meet, the woman explained this new "Systems of Care" concept to me. It meant that the whole system of S.R.S. would change their way of doing things. Child safety would remain the first priority, as it should be. But in the new systems of care approach, the main goal is to keep families together if at all possible.

I told her that I thought it was an excellent plan, but it was also the complete opposite of what they've been doing. I also went on to say that S.R.S. was never very good at following through and if they weren't willing to go all the way, I didn't want any part of it. Single mothers and families have been strung along for too long only to find out, often several years and up to ten case workers later, that once S.R.S. reaches their deadline to get things done, it's over. There is supposed to be a case plan that all involved have input into, but usually the worker is the one making the plan for your own and your children's futures, and that plan usually has to be completed in the time they set forth for you to complete.

I can't speak for others, but my experience is that an addict's life in recovery is never over. For those dealing with the system that are alcohol and drug addicted, *recovery is a process, not an event*! There's never a deadline in recovery. Addiction is the negative side of recovery, and recovery is the positive. And relapse is a part of recovery. You cannot relapse if you're not in recovery. And no two people are the same. Each case must be treated on an individual basis to be effective.

The woman from S.R.S. and I talked a lot about ourselves and our hopes for other families during that meeting, and we also cried. By the time the meeting was finished, I didn't care who she worked for, because I knew she was a good and caring woman no matter where she worked. I also knew before I left her that evening that I would accept the seat on this committee, but that I would tell her later.

Chapter Forty-Five

I am very happy to say that I believe in this new system that S.R.S. is bringing forth. And I also believe that with this new system in place, more families will be kept together. S.R.S. has become more willing to bring families to the table with them as partners, which is a big step from the way things used to be done, everything was on a "need to know" basis. The system that I partner with here in Kansas is very sincere in making these changes and following through.

I also believe that if all states would review, put into place and follow the system of care principles, there would be significant positive changes in the way states deal with families in trouble. One book that clearly describes the Systems of Care concepts and provides recommendations and examples of implementing Systems of Care is *A View From The Balcony: Leadership Challenges in Systems of Care* (De Carolis, 2005). This volume can serve as a guidebook to implement family-centered Systems Of Care. I'm sure there are other ways of working this out, but I as a Family Partner, in reading *A View From The Balcony*, rejoice and weep at the same time. I rejoice because there is a program and principles to follow that can and will, if adopted, change the child welfare system forever. And I weep for myself and others who did not have this system of care in place at the time of our journey through the child welfare system.

I accepted the seat on the Systems of Care Committee and I take this very seriously. I am there as a Family Partner to ensure that S.R.S. is doing what they promised and making the changes necessary as promised with this new way of doing business. Although I'm there in full support and as a voice for single mothers, I am also there in support of S.R.S. in their sincerity to make these changes. I believe that most of the workers are excited and eager to move forward in doing business differently. And I also believe there are those who aren't for this change, will soon weed themselves out, if they haven't already done so.

I am excited as well, and I can't say enough how much I fully support this new way of doing things. I think we should all be able to look into our hearts and forgive a system that has admitted publicly, "Hey we screwed up." No matter how late it is, they are making an honest effort to do things right.

I say to all single parents and to all parents who have ended up involved with S.R.S. (or whatever your own state child welfare system is called), "Here is your chance to take your lives back with the support of this new system - the ball is pretty much in your court." As a parent myself who was not given this opportunity, I can only hope and pray that wherever you are in your life's journey, you keep your children with you always and never have to wonder where they are and if they are well and happy. The last pictures I have of Sultan and Malachi are when they were four and five years old. How I wish I could know what has become of them.

If you live in a place where the System of Care approach is being implemented, don't rob yourself of what this new approach has to offer you and your children. One thing the new system will do is place more accountability on parents for the outcomes. I pray that you use it to your full advantage, as it has been put in place to help you.

Please look to God for forgiveness of the past mistakes made by this system and help them to do better, and make sure that the ball isn't dropped in another case, as occurred in mine. If you are reading this and going through something similar, give S.R.S. a chance to right the wrongs. I don't have any children to lose to this system anymore, and I gain nothing by supporting this program but peace of mind. I do this for every parent, mother, and child. I pray that they will never have to experience the pain and anguish that I feel daily where my children are concerned.

As long as God gives me breath, I will praise and thank Him for the opportunity I've been given to carry the message to those that still suffer. And to also give hope to those who can't believe that change is possible. I always remember that nothing is too great for God.

Chapter Forty-Six

Since the death of my grandfather, Ellsworth Boldridge, in 1993, my mother and her siblings had been estranged from each other. This is due to a dispute over his estate that he worked for his entire life, so that he and my grandmother could leave a legacy for their children and grandchildren. My grandfather was not only a farmer, he was a very astute businessman, and above all, he was a fair man. I loved him and miss him dearly. One thing that I remember him saying on several occasions was that we should "share and share alike." He believed in taking care of his family, and he didn't play favorites among his seven children and nineteen grandchildren. Yet, despite all of his emphasis on treating everyone fairly, his children, my mom and her siblings, have been in and out of court since shortly after his death. And nothing is settled yet.

Once I joined the church, I would stand at the door to usher and notice that my mom's sister sat on one side of the church and my mother on the other. Before and after church they hardly said two words to one another other. I wasn't sure what I was supposed to do, but I knew in my heart that the Lord would somehow use me to bring our family back together. At first I tried to deny it, and I thought, "Who's going to listen to me and take me seriously? " But I also know that when God wants us to move, we absolutely must.

About a month after I joined, my aunt was leaving church on Sunday and I told her I needed to talk to her. She invited me out to her house. When I got there, I told her about my strong feeling that God had placed in my heart that it was time to get this family together. I can't tell you what her thoughts were, but I will say that a look of relief was on her face. I was never very close to any of my aunts or they to me, but on that day we were able to agree on the fact that my grandfather wanted us to be close as a family and to enjoy as a family what he left us. I began a relationship with my aunt that day, and I'm glad for it.

I had been planning a picnic to be held on my grandparents' farm on July 4th, which was a few weeks after this. The picnic was in honor of my grandparents to celebrate the legacy they left us and to honor the two of them, who touched many lives in a positive way. My family, the Boldridges, had been nominated 2005 4-H Family of the Year, due to all the hard work and determination of my grandparents. They formed the Walnut Creek 4-H Club in Atchison County in 1965. Their goal was that all children, black and white, have the opportunity to learn and grow together. This was one of the first purposely integrated groups in this area. My grandparents believed in equality and families helping families no matter the color.

I called the picnic 4-H Family Fun Day, and hoped that many of those who had the opportunity to know my grandparents would come together and celebrate the life they led. This was also chance to get all of my relatives together. I mailed out fliers, not sure if anyone would show other than my mom and sisters and my aunt and her kids. We hadn't all been together like that for close to twenty years

It was getting close to the 4th of July, and I hadn't even been over to the farm in twenty five years or more. I decided to recreate it the way I last remembered it, so I built it on a piece of plywood. I had heard that it was rundown and nothing like it was the last time I was there. I worked day and night to get my model completed. I also wanted to surprise my mom and her sisters and hopefully spark some memories of what it used to be like there.

A week before the 4th, I had to go over there to the farm to decide where we would set up the picnic. It was so sad for me. I remember running around there as a little girl, without a care in the world. No matter whose farm I have visited since, none ever measured up to my grandpa's farm. They didn't even smell as good as his did.

On the day of the picnic, I was worried that almost no one would come. Only one person, a cousin, had called to say she would be there.

The party was to start at noon and end at 4:00 P.M. By 1:00, people started to show up. I had my display of the farm set up and my aunt had a 4-H display of all the siblings and my grandparents and their different achievements in 4-H. By 2:00, there were more than seventy-five people there. My pastor and his wife came and started us off with a prayer.

Everyone I invited showed up except one of my mom's sisters and a couple of cousins. But maybe they will come next year because that day, we decided that we'd do it again the following year. I hadn't seen my mom and sisters together in years; they laughed and talked and two of them even hugged. I can bet they've never done that before. This would be the first year at New Years that I've seen my mom and her sisters in the same house.

We've still got a ways to go. But I cannot imagine my life today without my sisters and my family in it. I'm grateful for where the Lord had brought me from. It hasn't been easy but it's a whole lot easier walking the road with Jesus instead of by myself. I pray that this book reaches all who are supposed to read it and even those who think they're not.

CONCLUSION

I now have a seat on not one but two statewide committees. Who would have thought I would be where I am today? One thing I do know is, if it's something the Lord puts before you to do, my best advice to you is to go ahead, even when you don't know how you will do it. In my experience, the Lord already has the plan in place to see you through.

As for my children, LaTesha graduated college last year with a B.A. in Social Work. Winsome began college in the fall, with plans to major in journalism She's very popular around campus and made it into Dynamic Praise, a world-renowned gospel group that began at the college she attends. Blake is a gifted musician and puts on concerts of Gospel Rap at various churches and functions far and wide. He's only sixteen years old and I don't think he's realized his full potential. Hearing him play the keyboards and drums, I can tell there's an amazing passion there for someone his age, and I will support him in whatever he decides to do. Philemon is unsure of what he wants or even likes to do, although he's very good at repairing things around the house, and enjoys playing football and basketball. But he's only fourteen years old, and I believe he's feeling his way.

The Lord has just recently blessed me with custody of my two year-old great nephew, LeHas. He is the son of my niece Brenda who stayed with me while she was pregnant with him. She had to go away for awhile, I cannot divulge where. But I believe this all worked out the way it did because God is giving me a second chance to raise a child. I'm also seeing what I missed out on with my own children. When his mother returns I will gladly but with sadness return LeHas to her. I believe that all children and their mothers should always have the chance to be together again.

Sultan and Malachi are still out there somewhere, and I have to trust and believe that the Lord has placed them where they are happy and loved. I know that my boys will be united with me again someday. The Lord takes care of those who serve Him. He promises to give us the desires of our hearts, and I know that in His time I will have mine.

Angela Braxton is available for speaking engagements and personal appearances. For more information contact Angela at:

ADVANTAGE BOOKS™
PO Box 160847
Altamonte Springs, FL 32716

Longwood, Florida, USA

"we bring dreams to life"™
www.advbookstore.com

Printed in the United States
59263LVS00007BB/7-12

9 781597 550970